150

TAPAS
recipes

D0184524

INSPIRED IDEAS FOR
EVERYDAY COOKING

CONTENTS

INTRODUCTION

Tapas, Spain's popular dining format, provides a wonderful way to share and enjoy a wide selection of fabulous fuss-free dishes with friends and family. Many typical tapas recipes are deliciously easy to make, with the focus being on flavour and appeal, so they are ideal for creating a fantastic feed-a-crowd supper.

Originally a selection of savoury appetizers or snacks served in Spanish bars, tapas have evolved to become a complete meal consisting of a wide variety of tempting small plates of food. Tapas can be cold or hot and these simple but sensational mix-and-match snacks are perfect for casual dining and easy entertaining.

This outstanding collection of recipes comprises an amazing choice of

tapas that is sure to set your senses ablaze. We feature popular classics plus some less familiar treats, including delicious dips, pâtés, pinchos, bites and puffs, tempting toasts, toasties, bruschetta and flatbread, as well as some sensational skewers, salads, soups and stuffed vegetables. There really is something for everyone. By choosing and combining a selection of these delightful dishes, you can create a fantastic feast of flavours and textures and bring a taste of Spain to your table.

First up is a tempting collection of bite-sized nibbles and snacks that are sure to whet your appetite, including some nourishing nuggets like Cracked Marinated Olives, Prawn & Chorizo Pinchos and Pork Belly Bites. Or, if cheese is your choice, select from tasty morsels such as Dates with Cheese & Ham, Cheese Puffs with Fiery Tomato Salsa and Sun-dried Tomato & Goat's Cheese Tarts.

Next on the menu is a marvellous medley of meat and poultry tapas, featuring some meaty mouthfuls that are bound to impress, such as Chorizo in Red Wine, Tiny Meatballs in Almond Sauce and Lamb Skewers with Lemon. If you prefer poultry, pick delights like Chicken Wings Chilindron, Chicken Rolls with Olives or Crispy Chicken & Ham Croquettes.

We feature a great choice of fish and seafood sensations next, including Deep-fried Whitebait, Seared Squid & Golden Potatoes and Tuna-stuffed Pepper Strips. Or, for something a bit more adventurous, choose from tempting dishes like mouthwatering Monkfish Bites with Green Sauce, Mixed Seafood Kebabs with Chilli & Lime Glaze or Marinated Sardine Fillets with Oregano & Fennel.

The next chapter concentrates on creative vegetable, cheese and egg-based tapas and includes classics like Potatas Bravas, Gazpacho and Mushrooms with Roasted Garlic & Spring Rolls, plus delicious easy eats such as Artichoke & Red Pepper Tortilla, Flamenco Eggs and Figs with Blue Cheese.

Finally, tantalize your taste buds with a collection of truly tasty toppings for breads and pastry fillings. Enjoy ever-popular dishes like Tapenade, Mixed Vegetable Bruschetta and Aubergine & Pepper Dip, or pick other temptations such as Russian Salad, Prawn & Haricot Toasties, Artichoke & Pimiento Flatbread and Potato & Spinach Triangles.

So, whether you're an aficionado or a culinary novice, this multitude of marvellous tapas provides you with the perfect opportunity to gather your guests round the table and celebrate Spain's wonderful way of sharing simple but sensational feel-good food.

When selecting which tapas to make and serve, be sure to choose a range of dishes with varying flavours, textures and colours, so you can create an appealing array for your companions. Choose some tapas with strong bold flavours to stimulate the palate and others with more subtle flavours, to make sure you satisfy all tastes, and remember to serve a selection of cold and hot tapas.

As you prepare and serve your tapas, the amazing aromas wafting from the kitchen are sure to draw your guests to the table, so encourage them to dip in and savour every mouthful as they munch their way through these delightful dishes.

INTRODUCTION

BITE-SIZED NIBBLES & SNACKS

COURGETTE FRITTERS WITH PINE NUT SAUCE

Serves: 6–8   **Prep: 25 mins**   **Cook: 15 mins**

Ingredients

3 tbsp plain flour

1 tsp paprika

1 large egg

2 tbsp milk

450 g/1 lb baby courgettes, cut diagonally into 5-mm/¼-inch slices

sunflower oil, for shallow-frying

sea salt, for sprinkling

Pine nut sauce

100 g/3½ oz pine nuts

1 garlic clove, peeled

3 tbsp Spanish extra virgin olive oil

1 tbsp lemon juice

3 tbsp water

1 tbsp chopped fresh flat-leaf parsley

salt and pepper

Method

1 To make the sauce, put the pine nuts and garlic into a food processor and process to form a purée. With the motor still running, gradually add the olive oil, lemon juice and water to form a smooth sauce.

2 Stir in the parsley and season to taste with salt and pepper. Transfer to a serving bowl and set aside.

3 Put the flour and paprika into a polythene bag and shake well.

4 Beat together the egg and milk in a large bowl.

5 Add the courgette slices to the flour mixture and toss until coated. Shake off the excess flour.

6 In a large frying pan, heat enough sunflower oil to come about 1 cm/½ inch up the side of the pan. Dip the courgette slices, one at a time, into the egg mixture, then put them into the hot oil.

7 Fry the courgette slices, in batches and in a single layer so that they do not overcrowd the pan, for 2 minutes, or until they are crisp and golden brown.

8 Using a slotted spoon, remove the fritters from the pan and drain on kitchen paper. Continue until all the courgette slices are cooked.

BITE-SIZED NIBBLES & SNACKS

9 Transfer the fritters to a serving platter. Sprinkle with a little sea salt, drizzle over the pine nut sauce and serve piping hot.

★ **Variation**

Replace the courgettes with slices of squash or marrow if you don't have a courgette to hand.

STUFFED OLIVES

Serves: 6   **Prep: 20-25 mins**   **Cook: N/A**

Ingredients

4 tbsp Spanish extra virgin olive oil

1 tbsp sherry vinegar, or to taste

2 tbsp very finely chopped parsley

finely grated rind of ½ orange

18 large stoned black olives

18 large stoned green olives

12 anchovy fillets in oil, drained

½ grilled red pepper in oil, drained and cut into 12 small pieces

12 blanched almonds

Method

1 Whisk together the oil, vinegar, parsley and orange rind in a small serving bowl, adding extra vinegar to taste. Set aside.

2 Make a lengthways slit in 12 of the black olives and 12 of the green olives without cutting all the way through.

3 Roll up the anchovy fillets and gently press them into the cavities of six of the slit green olives and six of the slit black olives.

4 Use the pieces of red pepper to stuff the remaining slit olives.

5 Slip a blanched almond into the centre of each of the remaining olives.

6 Add all the olives to the bowl of dressing and stir gently.

7 Serve with wooden cocktail sticks for spearing the olives.

CRACKED MARINATED OLIVES

Serves: 8

Prep: 20–25 mins,
plus standing
& marinating

Cook: N/A

Ingredients

450 g/1 lb can or jar
unstoned large green
olives, drained

4 garlic cloves, peeled

2 tsp coriander seeds

1 small lemon

4 sprigs of fresh thyme

4 feathery stalks of fennel

2 small fresh red chillies
(optional)

pepper

Spanish extra virgin olive oil,
to cover

Method

1 To allow the flavours of the marinade to penetrate the olives, place on a chopping board and, using a rolling pin, bash them lightly so that they crack slightly. Alternatively, use a sharp knife to cut a lengthways slit in each olive as far as the stone. Using the flat side of a broad knife, lightly crush each garlic clove. Using a pestle and mortar, crack the coriander seeds. Cut the lemon, with its rind, into small chunks.

2 Put the olives, garlic, coriander seeds, lemon chunks, thyme sprigs, fennel and chillies, if using, in a large bowl and toss together. Season with pepper to taste, but you should not need to add salt as conserved olives are usually salty enough. Pack the ingredients tightly into a glass jar with a lid. Pour in enough olive oil to cover the olives, then seal the jar tightly.

3 Leave the olives at room temperature for 24 hours, then marinate in the refrigerator for at least 1 week but preferably 2 weeks before serving. From time to time, gently give the jar a shake to re-mix the ingredients. Return the olives to room temperature and remove from the oil to serve. Provide cocktail sticks for spearing the olives.

CURED MEAT PLATTER WITH HERB SALAD

Serves: 8   **Prep: 20 mins**   **Cook: N/A**

Ingredients

4 ripe figs

125 g/4½ oz chorizo

125 g/4½ oz thinly sliced Iberico ham

125 g/4½ oz thinly sliced Serrano ham

125 g/4½ oz thinly sliced lomo

125 g/4½ oz thinly sliced salchichon

125 g/4½ oz thinly sliced cecina

3 tbsp extra virgin olive oil, plus extra to serve

2 tsp moscatel vinegar

6 tbsp fresh flat-leaf parsley leaves

1 tbsp fresh mint leaves

1 tbsp snipped fresh chives

salt and pepper

country-style bread, to serve

Method

1 Cut each fig into quarters lengthways. Arrange on one side of a large serving platter.

2 Remove and discard the casing from the chorizo. Thinly slice the chorizo, then transfer to the platter.

3 Arrange the remaining meats on the platter, keeping each variety separate.

4 Put the oil and moscatel vinegar into a bowl and season to taste with salt and pepper, then whisk until blended. Add the herbs and quickly toss together. Immediately transfer to the platter with the meats.

5 Serve with plenty of bread, and extra oil for dipping.

CHORIZO-STUFFED MUSHROOMS

Makes: 24

Prep: 25 mins,
plus standing

Cook: 20–25 mins

Ingredients

24 chestnut mushrooms,
each about 4 cm/
1½ inches in diameter

140 g/5 oz chorizo

1 tbsp Spanish olive oil,
plus extra for brushing

6 spring onions,
very finely chopped

¼ tsp Spanish
sweet paprika

80 g/2¾ oz fine dry
white breadcrumbs

finely grated rind of 1 lemon

2 tbsp very finely chopped
fresh parsley

salt and pepper

Method

1 Preheat the oven to 180°C/350°F/Gas Mark 4.
Brush a shallow roasting tin with oil. Remove the
stalks from the mushrooms and finely chop, then
set aside.

2 Lightly brush the mushrooms with oil. Lightly
season the inside of the mushrooms with salt and
pepper and set aside.

3 Remove and discard the casing from the
chorizo, then finely chop.

4 Add the chorizo to a dry frying pan over a
medium–high heat and fry, using a wooden
spoon to break it up, for 3–5 minutes, until it gives
off its fat. Transfer to a bowl using a slotted spoon,
leaving as much fat as possible in the pan.

5 Add the oil to the pan, then add the spring
onions, paprika and chopped mushroom stalks
and season to taste with salt and pepper. Fry,
stirring, for 3–5 minutes, until the onions are soft.

6 Add the onion mixture to the chorizo and stir in
the breadcrumbs, lemon rind and parsley.
Adjust the seasoning, adding salt and pepper
if needed.

7 Use a teaspoon to divide the mixture between the mushrooms, mounding it slightly. Arrange the mushrooms in a single layer in the prepared tin.

8 Bake in the preheated oven for 15 minutes, until tender. Carefully transfer the mushrooms to kitchen paper to drain. Leave to stand for 5 minutes.

9 Transfer the mushrooms to a serving platter and serve hot, warm or at room temperature.

SAUTÉED GARLIC MUSHROOMS

Serves: 6   **Prep: 15 mins**   **Cook: 10–15 mins**

Ingredients

450 g/1 lb button mushrooms

5 tbsp Spanish olive oil

2 garlic cloves, finely chopped

lemon juice, to taste

4 tbsp chopped fresh parsley

salt and pepper

lemon wedges, to garnish

country-style bread, to serve

Method

1 Halve or quarter any large mushrooms.

2 Heat the oil in a large frying pan. Add the garlic and fry for 30 seconds–1 minute, or until lightly browned.

3 Add the mushrooms and sauté over a high heat, stirring frequently, until they have absorbed the oil. Reduce the heat to low. When the juices have come out of the mushrooms, increase the heat and sauté for 4–5 minutes, stirring frequently, until the juices have almost evaporated.

4 Add a squeeze of lemon juice and season to taste with salt and pepper. Stir in the parsley and cook for a further minute.

5 Transfer to a warmed serving dish and garnish with lemon wedges. Serve with bread to mop up the juices.

BITE-SIZED NIBBLES & SNACKS

STUFFED EGGS WITH ANCHOVIES & CHEESE

Serves: 8

Prep: 25 mins,
plus cooling

Cook: 15–20 mins

Ingredients

8 eggs

50 g/1¾ oz canned
anchovy fillets in
olive oil, drained

55 g/2 oz Manchego
cheese, grated

4 tbsp Spanish extra virgin
olive oil

1 tbsp freshly squeezed
lemon juice

1 garlic clove, crushed

salt and pepper

4 stoned green Spanish
olives, halved to garnish

4 stoned black Spanish
olives, halved to garnish

hot or sweet smoked
Spanish paprika, for dusting

Method

1 Put the eggs in a saucepan, cover with cold water and slowly bring to the boil. Reduce the heat and simmer gently for 10 minutes. Immediately drain the eggs and rinse under cold running water to cool. Gently tap the eggs to crack the shells and leave until cold.

2 When the eggs are cold, crack the shells all over and remove them. Using a stainless steel knife, halve the eggs, carefully remove the egg yolks and put in a food processor.

3 Add the anchovy fillets, Manchego cheese, oil, lemon juice and garlic to the egg yolks and process to a purée. Season to taste with salt and pepper.

4 Using a teaspoon, spoon the mixture into the egg white halves. Alternatively, using a piping bag fitted with a 1-cm/½-inch plain nozzle, pipe the mixture into the egg white halves. Arrange the eggs in a serving dish, cover and chill in the refrigerator until ready to serve.

5 To serve, put an olive half on the top of each stuffed egg and dust with paprika.

BITE-SIZED NIBBLES & SNACKS

PRAWN & CHORIZO PINCHOS

Makes: 24   **Prep: 20–25 mins**   **Cook: 7 mins**

Ingredients

½ lemon, sliced

1 tbsp sea salt

24 large peeled, raw prawns, thawed if frozen

140 g/5 oz chorizo

24 fresh basil leaves

lemon wedges, to serve

Method

1 Bring a large saucepan of water to the boil with the lemon slices and salt.

2 Cut along the length of each prawn and remove and discard the dark vein. Set aside.

3 Remove and discard the casing from the chorizo, then cut it into 24 x 5-mm/¼-inch slices and set aside.

4 Add the prawns to the boiling water, reduce the heat to low and simmer for 1½–2 minutes, until the prawns turn pink and begin to curl.

5 Drain the prawns, then place under cold running water to stop the cooking. Pat dry with a clean tea towel.

6 Use a wooden cocktail stick to skewer a piece of chorizo, a basil leaf and then a prawn. Cover and chill until required.

7 Arrange on a serving plate and serve with lemon wedges for squeezing over.

STUFFED CHERRY TOMATOES

Makes: 24

Prep: 35 mins, plus draining

Cook: N/A

Ingredients

24 cherry tomatoes

Anchovy & olive filling

50 g/1¾ oz canned anchovy fillets in olive oil

8 pimiento-stuffed green Spanish olives, finely chopped

2 large hard-boiled eggs, finely chopped

pepper

Crab mayonnaise filling

170 g/6 oz canned crabmeat, drained

4 tbsp mayonnaise

1 tbsp chopped fresh flat-leaf parsley

salt and pepper

paprika, to garnish

Black olive & caper filling

12 stoned black Spanish olives

3 tbsp capers

6 tbsp Aïoli

salt and pepper

Method

1. If necessary, cut and discard a very thin slice from the stalk end of each tomato to make the bases flat and stable. Cut a thin slice from the smooth end of each cherry tomato and discard. Loosen the pulp and seeds of each and scoop out, discarding the flesh. Turn the scooped-out tomatoes upside down on kitchen paper and leave to drain for 5 minutes.

2. Drain the anchovies, reserving the olive oil for later, then chop finely and place in a bowl. Add the olives and hard-boiled eggs. Pour in a trickle of the reserved olive oil to moisten the mixture, then season with pepper. (Don't add salt as the anchovies are salty.) Mix well together.

3. Place the crabmeat, mayonnaise and parsley in a bowl and mix well together. Season the filling to taste with salt and pepper. Sprinkle with paprika before serving.

4. Place the olives and capers on kitchen paper to drain them well, then chop finely and place in a bowl. Add the aïoli and mix well together. Season the filling to taste with salt and pepper.

5. Fill a piping bag fitted with a 2-cm/¾-inch plain nozzle with the filling of your choice and use to fill the hollow tomato shells. Store the cherry tomatoes in the refrigerator until ready to serve.

BITE-SIZED NIBBLES & SNACKS

DATES WITH CHEESE & HAM

Makes: 24

Prep: 20 mins, plus cooling

Cook: 5–6 mins

Ingredients

24 large ready-to-eat dried dates

140 g/5 oz Manchego cheese

6 thin slices Serrano ham

Spanish olive oil, for brushing

Method

1. Using a small knife, slit each date and remove the stones, if necessary, then set aside.

2. Cut away the cheese rind, then cut the cheese into 24 equal-sized pieces that will fit in the dates, each about 5 mm/¼ inch thick.

3. Push the cheese inside the dates and close the dates around the cheese.

4. Cut each slice of ham into four long strips.

5. Wrap a strip of ham around each date and gently press the ham to seal.

6. Heat a frying pan over a very high heat. Brush the surface with oil, then use kitchen paper to wipe out the excess.

7. Working in batches, if necessary, add as many stuffed dates as will fit in the pan in a single layer and fry for 1–1½ minutes, until the ham is crisp.

8. Turn the dates and fry on the other side for a further minute, or until the cheese is soft and the ham is crisp.

9. Leave to cool for 2 minutes, then serve hot with wooden cocktail sticks for spearing the dates.

HOT ANCHOVY DIP WITH VEGETABLES

Serves: 8   **Prep: 15–20 mins**   **Cook: 5 mins**

Ingredients

100 g/3½ oz anchovy fillets in oil

4 large garlic cloves, unpeeled

sea salt

125 ml/4 fl oz Spanish extra virgin olive oil, plus extra if needed

sherry vinegar, to taste

pepper

selection of freshly prepared vegetables, such as chicory leaves, courgette slices and red pepper strips, to serve

Method

1 Drain the anchovy fillets, reserving the oil.

2 Finely chop the anchovies and transfer them with the reserved oil to a frying pan over a low heat.

3 Put the garlic cloves on a chopping board and bash with the side of a large cook's knife. Remove and discard the skins.

4 Very lightly sprinkle the garlic with salt and use the flat of the knife to crush the garlic into a paste.

5 Add the garlic paste and olive oil to the pan, increase the heat to medium–high and stir until the anchovies dissolve. Make sure that the garlic does not burn.

6 Add vinegar and pepper to taste.

7 Transfer to a serving dish and serve hot with a selection of freshly prepared vegetables for dipping.

CALAMARES FRITOS

Serves: 6 **Prep: 15 mins** **Cook: 15–20 mins**

Ingredients

450 g/1 lb prepared squid

plain flour, for dusting

sunflower oil, for deep-frying

sea salt

lemon wedges and Aïoli, to serve

Method

1 Slice the squid into 1-cm/½-inch rings and halve the tentacles if large.

2 Dust the squid with flour so that it is lightly coated.

3 Heat enough oil for deep-frying in a large saucepan or deep-fat fryer to 180–190°C/350–375°F, or until a cube of bread browns in 30 seconds. Carefully add the squid, in batches, and fry for 2–3 minutes, or until golden brown. Do not overcook.

4 Using a slotted spoon, remove the fried squid from the oil and drain well on kitchen paper. Keep hot in a warm oven while you fry the remaining squid.

5 Sprinkle the fried squid with sea salt. Serve piping hot with lemon wedges for squeezing over and aïoli for dipping.

BITE-SIZED NIBBLES & SNACKS

PICKLED STUFFED PEPPERS

Serves: 6

Prep: 15 mins,
plus chilling

Cook: N/A

Ingredients

200 g/7 oz Cuajada cheese, Queso del Tietar or other fresh goat's cheese

400 g/14 oz pickled peppers (or pimientos del piquillo), drained

1 tbsp finely chopped fresh dill

salt and pepper

Method

1 Cut the cheese into pieces about 1 cm/½ inch long. Slit the sides of the peppers and deseed, if you like. Stuff the peppers with the cheese.

2 Arrange the stuffed peppers on serving plates, sprinkle with the dill and season to taste with salt and pepper. Cover and chill until ready to serve.

BITE-SIZED NIBBLES & SNACKS

MARINATED AUBERGINES

Serves: 4

Prep: 20 mins,
plus marinating

Cook: 1 hour

Ingredients

2 aubergines, halved lengthways

salt and pepper

4 tbsp Spanish olive oil

2 garlic cloves, finely chopped

2 tbsp chopped fresh parsley

1 tbsp chopped fresh thyme

2 tbsp lemon juice

Method

1 Make 2–3 slashes in the flesh of the aubergine halves and place, cut-side down, in an ovenproof dish. Season to taste with salt and pepper, pour over the olive oil and sprinkle with the garlic, parsley and thyme. Cover and leave to marinate at room temperature for 2–3 hours.

2 Preheat the oven to 180°C/350°F/Gas Mark 4. Uncover the dish and roast the aubergines in the preheated oven for 45 minutes. Remove the dish from the oven and turn the aubergines over. Baste with the cooking juices and sprinkle with the lemon juice. Return to the oven and cook for a further 15 minutes.

3 Transfer the aubergines to serving plates. Spoon over the cooking juices and serve hot or warm.

BITE-SIZED NIBBLES & SNACKS

SIZZLING CHILLI PRAWNS

Serves: 6   **Prep: 15 mins**   **Cook: 5 mins**

Ingredients

500 g/1 lb 2 oz large
raw prawns

6 tbsp Spanish olive oil

2 garlic cloves,
finely chopped

1 small fresh red chilli,
deseeded and
finely chopped

pinch of paprika

pinch of salt

crusty bread, to serve

Method

1 Peel the prawns, removing the heads but leaving
the tails intact. Cut along the length of each
prawn and remove and discard the dark vein.

2 Rinse the prawns under cold running water and
pat dry on kitchen paper.

3 Heat the oil in a large frying pan until quite hot,
then add the garlic and fry for 30 seconds.

4 Add the prawns, chilli, paprika and salt and
fry for 2–3 minutes, stirring constantly, until the
prawns turn pink and begin to curl.

5 Transfer to a serving dish and serve with bread to
mop up the juices.

BITE-SIZED NIBBLES & SNACKS

FRIED MANCHEGO CHEESE

Makes: 6   **Prep: 15–20 mins**   **Cook: 12 mins**

Ingredients

200 g/7 oz Manchego cheese

3 tbsp plain flour

1 egg

1 tsp water

85 g/3 oz fresh white or brown breadcrumbs

sunflower oil, for deep-frying

salt and pepper

Method

1 Cut the cheese into six triangles, each about 1 cm/½ inch thick.

2 Place the flour in a polythene bag and season to taste with salt and pepper.

3 Break the egg into a shallow dish, add the water and beat together.

4 Spread out the breadcrumbs on a large plate.

5 Toss the cheese pieces in the flour so that they are evenly coated.

6 Dip the cheese in the egg mixture, then roll it in the breadcrumbs so that the pieces are coated on all sides.

7 Heat enough oil for deep-frying in a large, heavy-based frying pan or deep-fat fryer to 180–190°C/350–375°F, or until a cube of bread browns in 30 seconds. Add the cheese and fry for 1–2 minutes, until golden brown.

8 Using a slotted spoon, remove the fried cheese and drain well on kitchen paper. Serve immediately.

CHEESE PUFFS WITH FIERY TOMATO SALSA

Serves: 8

Prep: 20–25 mins, plus chilling

Cook: 35–45 mins

Ingredients

70 g/2½ oz plain flour

50 ml/2 fl oz Spanish olive oil

150 ml/5 fl oz water

2 eggs, beaten

55 g/2 oz Manchego, Parmesan, Cheddar, Gouda or Gruyère cheese, finely grated

½ tsp paprika

salt and pepper

sunflower oil, for deep-frying

Fiery tomato salsa

2 tbsp Spanish olive oil

1 small onion, finely chopped

1 garlic clove, crushed

splash of dry white wine

400 g/14 oz canned chopped tomatoes

1 tbsp tomato purée

¼–½ tsp chilli flakes

dash of Tabasco sauce

pinch of sugar

salt and pepper

Method

1 To make the salsa, heat the olive oil in a saucepan. Add the onion and fry for 5 minutes, or until softened but not browned. Add the garlic and fry for a further 30 seconds. Add the wine and allow to bubble, then add all the remaining salsa ingredients to the saucepan and simmer, uncovered, for 10–15 minutes, or until a thick sauce has formed. Spoon into a serving bowl and reserve until ready to serve.

2 Meanwhile, prepare the cheese puffs. Sift the flour on to a plate or sheet of greaseproof paper. Place the olive oil and water in a saucepan and slowly bring to the boil. As soon as the water boils remove from the heat and quickly add the flour all at once. Using a wooden spoon, beat the mixture until it is smooth and leaves the sides of the saucepan.

3 Leave the mixture to cool for 1–2 minutes, then gradually add the eggs, beating hard after each addition and keeping the mixture stiff. Add the cheese and paprika, season to taste with salt and pepper and mix well. Store in the refrigerator until you are ready to fry the cheese puffs.

4 Just before serving the cheese puffs, heat the sunflower oil in a deep-fat fryer to 180–190°C/350–375°F, or until a cube of bread browns in 30 seconds. Drop teaspoonfuls of the prepared mixture, in batches, into the hot oil and deep-fry for 2–3 minutes, turning once, or until golden brown and crispy. They should rise to the surface of the oil and puff up. Drain well on kitchen paper.

5 Serve the puffs piping hot, accompanied by the fiery salsa for dipping and wooden cocktail sticks to spear the puffs.

CHILLIES RELLENOS

Serves: 4 **Prep: 25 mins** **Cook: 16–18 mins**

Ingredients

3 eggs, separated

55 g/2 oz plain flour

325 g/11½ oz Cheddar cheese

16 fresh green jalapeño chillies

sunflower oil or corn oil, for deep-frying

Method

1 Whisk the egg whites in a dry, grease-free bowl until stiff.

2 Beat the egg yolks in a separate bowl, then fold in the whites.

3 Spread out the flour in a shallow dish.

4 Cut 225 g/8 oz of the cheese into 16 sticks and grate the remainder.

5 Make a slit in the side of each chilli and scrape out the seeds. Rinse the cavities and pat dry with kitchen paper.

6 Place a stick of cheese inside each chilli. Preheat the grill. Heat enough oil for deep-frying in a large saucepan or deep-fat fryer to 180–190°C/350–375°F, or until a cube of bread browns in 30 seconds.

7 Dip the chillies in the egg mixture, then in the flour. Deep-fry, turning occasionally, until golden brown all over. Drain well on kitchen paper.

8 Arrange the chillies in a baking dish and sprinkle over the grated cheese. Place under the preheated grill until the cheese has melted.

9 Serve immediately while still hot.

DEVILLED EGGS

Makes: 16   **Prep: 25–30 mins**   **Cook: 15–20 mins**

Ingredients

8 large eggs

2 whole canned or bottled pimientos del piquillo

16 stoned green Spanish olives

5 tbsp mayonnaise

8 drops of hot pepper sauce

large pinch of cayenne pepper

salt and pepper

Little Gem lettuce leaves, to serve

Spanish paprika, to garnish

Method

1 Put the eggs into a saucepan, cover with cold water and slowly bring to the boil. Reduce the heat to very low, cover and simmer gently for 10 minutes. Drain the eggs and place under cold running water until they are cold.

2 Crack the eggshells and remove. Halve the eggs lengthways, then carefully remove the yolks.

3 Place the yolks in a sieve set over a bowl and rub through, then mash with a fork.

4 Place the pimientos on kitchen paper to dry well, then finely chop, reserving 16 small strips. Finely chop half the olives. Halve the remaining olives. Add the chopped pimientos and chopped olives to the mashed egg yolks. Add the mayonnaise, mix together well, then add the hot pepper sauce, cayenne pepper, and salt and pepper to taste.

5 Use a teaspoon to spoon a little of the egg yolk mixture into the hollow in each egg white half. Add a small strip of the reserved pimientos and an olive half to the top of each stuffed egg.

6 Line a platter with lettuce leaves and arrange the eggs on top. Dust with a little paprika and serve.

BITE-SIZED NIBBLES & SNACKS

MELON, CHORIZO & ARTICHOKE SALAD

Serves: 8

Prep: 35–40 mins, plus cooling

Cook: 6 mins

Ingredients

12 small globe artichokes

juice of ½ lemon

2 tbsp Spanish olive oil

1 small orange-fleshed melon, such as cantaloupe

200 g/7 oz chorizo, outer casing removed

fresh tarragon or flat-leaf parsley sprigs, to garnish

Dressing

3 tbsp Spanish extra virgin olive oil

1 tbsp red wine vinegar

1 tsp prepared mustard

1 tbsp chopped fresh tarragon

salt and pepper

Method

1 To prepare the artichokes, cut off the stalks. With your hands, break off the toughest outer leaves at the base until the tender inside leaves are visible. Using a pair of scissors, cut the spiky tips off the leaves. Using a sharp knife, pare the dark green skin from the base and down the stem. As you prepare them, brush the cut surfaces of the artichokes with lemon juice to prevent discoloration. Alternatively, you could fill a bowl with cold water to which you have added a little lemon juice, and immerse the artichokes in the acidulated water to stop discoloration. Carefully remove the choke (the mass of silky hairs) by pulling it out with your fingers or by scooping it out with a spoon. It is very important to remove all the choke as the little barbs, if eaten, can irritate the throat. However, if you are using very young artichokes, you do not need to worry about removing the choke and you can include the stalk too, well scraped, as it will be quite tender. Cut the artichokes into quarters and brush them again with lemon juice.

2 Heat the olive oil in a large, heavy-based frying pan. Add the prepared artichokes and fry, stirring

frequently, for 5 minutes, or until the artichoke leaves are golden brown. Remove from the frying pan, transfer to a large serving bowl and leave to cool.

3 To prepare the melon, cut in half and scoop out the seeds with a spoon. Cut the flesh into bite-sized cubes. Add to the cooled artichokes. Cut the chorizo into bite-sized chunks and add to the melon and artichokes.

4 To make the dressing, place all the ingredients in a small bowl and whisk together. Just before serving, pour the dressing over the prepared salad ingredients and toss together. Serve the salad garnished with tarragon or parsley sprigs.

SUN-DRIED TOMATO & GOAT'S CHEESE TARTS

Serves: 6

Prep: 25 mins, plus cooling

Cook: 20-25 mins

Ingredients

70 g/2½ oz sun-dried tomatoes in oil, drained and 2 tbsp oil reserved

1 courgette, thinly sliced

1 garlic clove, crushed

250 g/9 oz puff pastry, thawed if frozen

plain flour, for dusting

150 g/5½ oz soft goat's cheese

salt and pepper

Method

1 Preheat the oven to 220°C/425°F/Gas Mark 7. Dampen a large baking sheet. Finely chop the sun-dried tomatoes and reserve. Heat 1 tablespoon of the reserved oil from the tomatoes in a large frying pan, add the courgette slices and cook over a medium heat, stirring occasionally, for 8–10 minutes until golden brown on both sides. Add the garlic and cook, stirring, for 30 seconds. Remove from the heat and leave to cool while you prepare the pastry bases.

2 Thinly roll out the pastry on a lightly floured work surface. Using a plain, 9-cm/3½-inch cutter, cut out 12 rounds, re-rolling the trimmings as necessary. Transfer the rounds to the prepared baking sheet and prick 3–4 times with the tines of a fork. Divide the courgette mixture equally among the pastry rounds, add the tomatoes, leaving a 1-cm/½-inch border around the edge, and top each tart with a spoonful of goat's cheese. Drizzle over 1 tablespoon of the remaining oil from the tomatoes and season to taste with salt and pepper.

3 Bake the tarts in the preheated oven for 10–15 minutes until golden brown and well risen. Serve warm.

SALT COD FRITTERS WITH SPINACH

Serves: 6

Prep: 30–35 mins, plus soaking & standing

Cook: 1 hour 5 mins– 1 hour 25 mins

Ingredients

250 g/9 oz dried salt cod in 1 piece

140 g/5 oz plain flour

1 tsp baking powder

¼ tsp salt

1 large egg, lightly beaten

100–150 ml/3½–5 fl oz milk

2 lemon slices

2 fresh parsley sprigs

1 bay leaf

½ tbsp garlic-flavoured olive oil

85 g/3 oz fresh baby spinach, rinsed

¼ tsp Spanish paprika

Spanish olive oil, for shallow-frying

sea salt, for sprinkling

Aïoli, to serve

Method

1 Put the salt cod into a large bowl, cover with cold water and leave to soak for 48 hours, changing the water at least three times a day.

2 Sift the flour, baking powder and salt into a large bowl and make a well. Mix the egg with 100 ml/3½ fl oz of the milk and pour into the well, stirring to make a smooth batter with a thick coating consistency. If it seems too thick, gradually stir in the remaining milk. Leave to stand for at least 1 hour.

3 Drain the salt cod and transfer to a large frying pan. Add the lemon slices, parsley sprigs, bay leaf and enough water to cover and bring to the boil. Reduce the heat and simmer for 30–45 minutes, until the fish is tender and flakes easily.

4 Meanwhile, heat the garlic-flavoured oil in a small saucepan over a medium heat. Add the spinach with just the water clinging to the leaves and cook for 3–4 minutes, until wilted.

5 Drain the spinach in a sieve, using the back of a spoon to press out any excess liquid. Finely chop the spinach, then stir it into the batter with the paprika.

6 Remove the fish from the water and flake, removing all the skin and bones. Stir the fish into the batter.

7 Heat enough olive oil for shallow-frying in a large frying pan. Use a greased tablespoon to drop spoonfuls of the batter into the oil and fry for 8–10 minutes, until golden brown. Work in batches to avoid overcrowding the pan.

8 Use a slotted spoon to transfer the fritters to kitchen paper to drain.

9 Sprinkle with sea salt and serve hot or at room temperature with aïoli for dipping.

DEEP-FRIED GREEN CHILLIES

Serves: 4-6   **Prep: 10 mins**   **Cook: 10 mins**

Ingredients

Spanish olive oil, for frying

250 g/9 oz sweet or hot
fresh green chillies

sea salt

Method

1 Heat 7.5 cm/3 inches of olive oil in a large,
heavy-based saucepan until it reaches
180–190°C/350–375°F, or until a cube of bread
turns brown in 30 seconds.

2 Rinse the chillies and pat them very dry with
kitchen paper. Drop them in the hot oil for no
longer than 20 seconds, or until they turn bright
green and the skins blister.

3 Remove with a slotted spoon and drain well on
crumpled kitchen paper. Sprinkle with sea salt
and serve immediately.

BITE-SIZED NIBBLES & SNACKS

DEEP-FRIED ARTICHOKE HEARTS

Serves: 4-6　　**Prep: 30-35 mins**　　**Cook: 30-35 mins**

Ingredients

50 g/2¼ oz self-raising flour

¼ tsp salt

¼ tsp hot or sweet smoked Spanish paprika

1 garlic clove, crushed

5 tbsp water

1 tbsp Spanish olive oil

juice of ½ lemon

12 small globe artichokes

sunflower or Spanish olive oil, for deep-frying

Aïoli, to serve

Method

1 To make the batter, put the flour, salt, paprika and garlic in a large bowl and make a well in the centre. Gradually pour the water and olive oil into the well and mix in the flour mixture from the side, beating constantly, until all the flour is incorporated and a smooth batter forms. Leave to rest while preparing the artichokes.

2 Fill a bowl with cold water and add the lemon juice. Cut off the stalks of the artichokes. With your hands, break off all the leaves and carefully remove the choke by pulling it out with your fingers or scooping it out with a spoon. Immediately put the artichoke hearts in the acidulated water to prevent discoloration.

3 Cook the artichoke hearts in a saucepan of boiling salted water for 15 minutes, or until tender, then drain well and pat dry with kitchen paper.

4 Heat the sunflower or olive oil in a deep-fat fryer to 180–190°C/350–375°F, or until a cube of bread browns in 30 seconds. Spear an artichoke heart on a cocktail stick, dip into the batter and then drop the artichoke heart and cocktail stick into the hot oil. Cook the artichoke hearts, in batches, for 1–2 minutes until golden brown and crisp. Remove and drain on kitchen paper.

5 Serve hot, with a bowl of Aïoli for dipping.

BITE-SIZED NIBBLES & SNACKS

PORK BELLY BITES

Serves: 8

Prep: 30 mins,
plus cooling & chilling

Cook: 6 hours 20 mins

Ingredients

900 g/2 lb boneless pork belly, skin scored

2 fennel bulbs, trimmed and halved

8 black peppercorns, crushed

4 garlic cloves, sliced

125 ml/4 fl oz dry white wine

salt

romesco sauce, to serve

Method

1 Preheat the oven to 150°C/300°F/Gas Mark 2. Put the pork, skin-side up, into a large flameproof casserole. Add the fennel, peppercorns, garlic and wine, and season to taste with salt.

2 Pour over enough water to cover the pork. Bring to the boil, then cover and transfer to the preheated oven. Cook for 5½ hours, until the pork is tender. Remove from the oven, take off the lid and leave the pork to cool in the cooking liquid for 30 minutes.

3 Carefully transfer the pork to a chopping board that will fit in the refrigerator. Discard the cooking liquid. Cover the pork with a baking sheet and put several food cans on top. Leave the pork to cool completely. Transfer to the refrigerator and leave overnight. Preheat the oven to 180°C/350°F/Gas Mark 4. Line a baking sheet with baking paper. Very carefully trim the pork and cut into bite-sized pieces.

4 Put as many pork pieces as will fit, skin-side down, into a non-stick frying pan and fry for 6–8 minutes, until the fat runs. Increase the heat to medium–high and fry for a further 5 minutes, until the skin is crisp and brown. Repeat with any remaining pieces.

Transfer the pork to the prepared baking sheet, skin-side up. Roast in the preheated oven for 20 minutes, until hot. Transfer the pork to a serving plate and spear with wooden cocktail sticks. Serve hot with romesco sauce for dipping.

AÏOLI

**Makes: about
350 ml/12 fl oz**

Prep: 15 mins,
plus optional chilling

Cook: N/A

Ingredients

3–4 large garlic cloves,
or to taste

pinch of sea salt

2 large egg yolks

1 tsp lemon juice

300 ml/10 fl oz Spanish extra
virgin olive oil

salt and pepper

Method

1 Put the garlic cloves into a mortar with the sea salt and mash to a paste with a pestle.

2 Put the paste in a food processor, add the egg yolks and lemon juice and process.

3 With the motor still running, slowly dribble in the oil through the feed tube until an emulsion forms and the sauce thickens.

4 Taste and adjust the seasoning, adding salt and pepper if needed. Serve immediately, or cover and chill for up to 3 days.

5 Bring to room temperature before serving as an accompaniment to a range of tapas dishes.

ROMESCO SAUCE

**Makes: about
300 ml/10 fl oz**

Prep: 20 mins,
plus soaking & standing

Cook: 20 mins

Ingredients

4 large, ripe tomatoes

16 blanched almonds

3 large garlic
cloves, unpeeled

1 dried sweet chilli, such as
ñora, soaked in water for
20 minutes and patted dry

4 dried red chillies, soaked
in water for 20 minutes
and patted dry

pinch of sugar

150 ml/5 fl oz Spanish
extra virgin olive oil

1½ tbsp sherry vinegar,
or to taste

salt and pepper

Method

1 Preheat the oven to 180°C/350°F/Gas Mark 4.
Put the tomatoes, almonds and garlic in a
roasting tin and roast in the preheated oven
for 20 minutes. Check the almonds after
about 7 minutes because they can burn
quickly; remove from the oven as soon as they
are golden.

2 Peel the roasted garlic and tomatoes, then put
them into a food processor with the soaked
sweet chilli and red chillies and process until
finely chopped.

3 Add the almonds and sugar and process again.

4 With the motor running, slowly add the oil
through the feed tube.

5 Add the vinegar and process briefly. Add extra
vinegar and salt and pepper to taste.

6 Leave to stand for at least 2 hours, or cover and
chill for up to 3 days.

7 Bring to room temperature and stir in any oil that
has separated. Serve as an accompaniment to
a range of tapas dishes.

SALTED ALMONDS

Serves: 6–8   **Prep: 15 mins**   **Cook: 20 mins**

Ingredients

4 tbsp Spanish olive oil

225 g/8 oz whole blanched almonds

sea salt

1 tsp Spanish sweet paprika

Method

1 Preheat the oven to 180°C/350°F/Gas Mark 4. Place the oil in a roasting tin and swirl it around to cover the base. Add the almonds and toss so that they are evenly coated in the oil, then spread them out in a single layer.

2 Roast the almonds in the preheated oven for 20 minutes, or until they are light golden brown, tossing several times during the cooking.

3 Drain the almonds on kitchen paper, then transfer them to a bowl.

4 While the almonds are still warm, sprinkle with plenty of sea salt and paprika and toss together to coat.

5 Serve the almonds warm or cold – they are at their best when served freshly cooked.

★ **Variation**

For a smoky, more earthy alternative use smoked paprika instead.

MEAT & POULTRY DISHES

CHICKEN LIVER PÂTÉ

Serves: 6

Prep: 25 mins,
plus cooling and chilling

Cook: 10–12 mins

Ingredients

225 g/8 oz chicken livers

140 g/5 oz butter

2 garlic cloves, coarsely chopped

2 tsp chopped fresh sage leaves

2 tbsp Marsala wine

150 ml/5 fl oz double cream

salt and pepper

55 g/2 oz butter and 4–6 fresh sage leaves, to garnish

Method

1 Trim the chicken livers and chop coarsely. Melt 55 g/2 oz of the butter in a heavy-based frying pan. Add the chicken livers and cook over a medium heat for 5–8 minutes until browned all over but still pink inside. Remove the pan from the heat.

2 Transfer the chicken livers, in small batches, to the blender and process. Return all the livers to the blender and add the garlic, sage leaves and remaining butter. Season with salt and pepper.

3 Pour the Marsala into the frying pan and stir with a wooden spoon, scraping up any sediment, then add the mixture to the blender. Process until the pâté is smooth and thoroughly mixed. Add the cream and process again to mix.
Spoon the pâté into individual pots and leave to cool completely.

4 Melt the butter for the garnish in a small saucepan over a low heat. Remove the pan from the heat and pour the melted butter over the surface of the cooled pâté. Arrange the sage leaves on top. Leave to cool, then cover with clingfilm and chill for at least 1 hour.

★ **Variation**

Duck livers can be used as an alternative to chicken livers.

CHARGRILLED LAMB CHOPS & PEPPERS

Serves: 8

Prep: 25–30 mins, plus marinating

Cook: 25–40 mins

Ingredients

4 tbsp Spanish olive oil, plus extra for brushing

2 tbsp red wine vinegar or sherry vinegar

2 large garlic cloves, finely chopped

1 tbsp sugar

1 tbsp chopped fresh thyme leaves

2 tsp chopped fresh oregano leaves

16 rib chops, ribs well trimmed

4 red peppers, deseeded and quartered

salt and pepper

Method

1 Combine the oil, vinegar, garlic, sugar, thyme and oregano in a large, non-metallic bowl. Add the lamb chops and rub with the mixture. Cover and leave to marinate at room temperature for up to 2 hours.

2 Heat a ridged, cast-iron griddle pan over a high heat until very hot. Brush with oil, then add the pepper quarters, skin-sides down, and chargrill for 12–15 minutes, until tender.

3 Peel off and discard the skins from the peppers, then cut the flesh into thin strips and set aside.

4 Reheat the pan. Season the lamb chops with salt and pepper. Working in batches, chargrill the lamb chops, turning once, for 5–8 minutes for medium.

5 Arrange the red pepper strips on a serving platter and top with the lamb chops. Serve hot, warm or at room temperature.

ANDALUSIAN PORK SKEWERS

Makes: 16

Prep: 30 mins, **Cook: 20 mins**
plus marinating & soaking

Ingredients

900 g/2 lb boneless lean pork loin chops, about 1 cm/½ inch thick

2 large garlic cloves, finely chopped

2 tsp Spanish sweet paprika

2 tsp ground cumin

¼ tsp ground cinnamon

pinch of cayenne pepper, or to taste

4 tbsp Spanish olive oil, plus extra for brushing

2 tsp tomato purée

1 green pepper, deseeded and cut into 16 squares

salt and pepper

lemon wedges, to serve

Method

1 Cut the pork into 32 bite-sized pieces.

2 Combine the garlic, paprika, cumin, cinnamon, cayenne pepper, and salt and pepper to taste in a large bowl. Stir in the oil and tomato purée.

3 Add the pork and rub the marinade into the meat. Cover and chill for at least 8 hours or overnight.

4 About 30 minutes before cooking, soak 16 wooden short skewers in cold water. Preheat the grill to high and brush the grill pan with oil.

5 Bring a saucepan of water to the boil. Add the green pepper pieces and blanch for 1 minute. Drain and rinse under cold running water. Pat dry and set aside.

6 Thread a piece of pork onto a cocktail stick, then add a piece of green pepper and another piece of pork. Repeat to make 16 skewers.

7 Arrange the skewers on the prepared grill pan and brush with any remaining marinade.

8 Grill for 12–15 minutes, turning frequently, until the pork is cooked through and lightly charred.

9 Serve immediately with lemon wedges for squeezing over.

CHORIZO & BROAD BEANS

Serves: 4 **Prep: 30–35 mins** **Cook: 15–20 mins**

Ingredients

1 kg/2 lb 4 oz fresh broad beans, shelled, or 350 g/12 oz frozen broad beans

250 g/9 oz chorizo

2 tbsp finely chopped fresh parsley

salt and pepper

Spanish extra virgin olive oil and crusty bread, to serve

Method

1 Bring a saucepan of lightly salted water to the boil over a high heat. Add the broad beans, bring back to the boil and cook for 5–8 minutes for fresh beans, or for 4–5 minutes for frozen beans, until tender.

2 Meanwhile, cut the chorizo in half lengthways. Remove and discard the casing, then thinly slice.

3 Drain the beans and immediately transfer them to a bowl of iced water. Use your fingers to pop the beans out of their skins, then pat dry and set aside.

4 Put the chorizo into a dry frying pan over a medium–high heat and cook, stirring, for 3–5 minutes, until it gives off its fat. Add the beans and stir until heated through. Stir in the parsley and season to taste with salt and pepper.

5 Transfer to a serving bowl and drizzle with extra virgin olive oil. Serve hot or at room temperature with plenty of bread.

PAELLA-STUFFED TOMATOES

Makes: 16 **Prep: 25–30 mins** **Cook: 40–50 mins, plus standing**

Ingredients

large pinch of saffron threads

500 ml/18 fl oz chicken stock

100 g/3½ oz chorizo

1 onion, finely chopped

4 large garlic cloves, finely chopped

250 g/9 oz skinless, boneless chicken thighs, finely diced

125 g/4½ oz fine French beans, trimmed and finely chopped

1 yellow pepper, deseeded and finely chopped

2 tsp Spanish hot paprika

250 g/9 oz Spanish paella rice

16 tomatoes

salt and pepper

Method

1 Put the saffron in a dry frying pan and toast over a high heat, stirring, for 30 seconds–1 minute, until it is giving off its aroma. Immediately tip it into a saucepan, add the stock and bring to the boil. Remove from the heat, cover and set aside.

2 Remove and discard the casing from the chorizo and finely dice.

3 Add the chorizo to a large dry frying pan over a high heat and fry, stirring, for 3–5 minutes, until it gives off its fat.

4 Add the onion and garlic to the pan. Reduce the heat and fry, stirring occasionally, for 5–8 minutes, until soft. Add the chicken, French beans, yellow pepper and paprika and stir for a further 2 minutes.

5 Add the rice and gently stir until it is coated with the oil. Pour in the stock and saffron mixture, season to taste with salt and pepper and bring to the boil without stirring.

6 Reduce the heat to very low and simmer for 20–25 minutes, uncovered, until the rice is tender and all the liquid has been absorbed. Shake the pan occasionally but do not stir.

7 Meanwhile, cut a very thin sliver off the bottom of each tomato, so it can stand upright. Cut off the tops and use a small spoon to scoop out and discard the seeds. Sprinkle with salt and leave to drain upside down.

8 Leave the paella to stand for 5 minutes, then spoon it into the tomato shells.

9 Arrange the tomatoes upright on a serving dish and serve hot or at room temperature.

SPICY FRIED BREAD & CHORIZO

Serves: 6–8　　　**Prep: 20 mins**　　　**Cook: 6–8 mins**

Ingredients

200 g/7 oz chorizo, outer casing removed

4 thick slices 2-day-old country bread

Spanish olive oil, for pan-frying

3 garlic cloves, finely chopped

fresh parsley sprigs and paprika, to garnish

Method

1 Cut the chorizo into 1-cm/½-inch thick slices and cut the bread, with its crusts still on, into 1-cm/½-inch cubes.

2 Add enough olive oil to a large, heavy-based frying pan to generously cover the base. Heat the oil, add the garlic and fry for 30 seconds– 1 minute, or until lightly browned.

3 Add the bread cubes to the pan and fry, stirring constantly, until golden brown and crisp. Add the chorizo slices and fry for 1–2 minutes, or until hot. Using a slotted spoon, remove the bread cubes and chorizo from the frying pan and drain well on kitchen paper.

4 Turn the fried bread and chorizo into a warmed serving bowl and toss together. Garnish the dish with parsley sprigs and a sprinkling of paprika and serve warm. Accompany with wooden cocktail sticks so that a piece of sausage and a cube of bread can be speared together for eating.

CHICKPEAS & CHORIZO

Serves: 4   **Prep: 15–20 mins**   **Cook: 8–10 mins**

Ingredients

250 g/9 oz chorizo in 1 piece, outer casing removed

4 tbsp Spanish olive oil

1 onion, finely chopped

1 large garlic clove, crushed

400 g/14 oz canned chickpeas, drained and rinsed

6 pimientos del piquillo, drained, patted dry and sliced

1 tbsp sherry vinegar, or to taste

salt and pepper

fresh parsley, chopped, to garnish

crusty bread, to serve

Method

1 Cut the chorizo into 1-cm/½-inch dice. Heat the oil in a large, heavy-based frying pan over a medium heat. Add the onion and garlic and fry, stirring occasionally, until the onion is softened but not browned. Stir in the chorizo and fry until heated through.

2 Transfer the mixture to a bowl and stir in the chickpeas and pimientos. Splash with sherry vinegar and season to taste with salt and pepper. Serve hot or at room temperature, generously sprinkled with parsley, with plenty of crusty bread.

MEAT & POULTRY DISHES

CHICKEN WINGS CHILINDRON

Makes: 16   **Prep: 20 mins**   **Cook: 50–60 mins**

Ingredients

16 chicken wings,
wing tips cut off

4 tbsp Spanish olive oil

1 large onion,
finely chopped

1 large green and 1 large
red pepper, deseeded
and chopped

100 g/3½ oz Serrano
ham, diced

4 large garlic cloves,
finely chopped

800 g/1 lb 12 oz canned
chopped tomatoes

2 bay leaves

1 tbsp dried thyme

125 ml/4 fl oz water

1 tsp Spanish hot paprika

salt and pepper

Method

1 Season the chicken wings with salt and pepper. Heat the oil in a large, heavy-based frying pan over a medium heat, then add the chicken wings, in batches, and fry on both sides until golden brown. Remove from the pan and set aside.

2 Add the onion, peppers, ham and garlic to the pan and cook for 5–8 minutes, until the onion is soft.

3 Stir in the tomatoes, bay leaves, thyme and water and season with salt and pepper. Bring to the boil, then reduce the heat, cover and simmer for 15 minutes, stirring occasionally.

4 Stir in the paprika and chicken wings, making sure they are covered with the sauce. Cover and simmer for 15–20 minutes, until the chicken wings are tender and the juices run clear when a skewer is inserted into the thickest part of the meat.

5 Transfer to a large serving platter and serve immediately.

SIRLOIN STEAK WITH GARLIC & SHERRY

Serves: 6-8

Prep: 15 mins,
plus marinating

Cook: 5-6 mins

Ingredients

4 sirloin steaks, about
175–225 g/6–8 oz each and
2.5 cm/1 inch thick

5 garlic cloves

salt and pepper

3 tbsp Spanish olive oil

125 ml/4 fl oz
dry sherry

chopped fresh flat-leaf
parsley, to garnish

crusty bread, to serve

Method

1 Cut the steaks into 2.5-cm/1-inch cubes and put in a large, shallow dish. Slice 3 of the garlic cloves and set aside. Finely chop the remaining garlic cloves and sprinkle over the steak cubes. Season generously with pepper and mix together well. Cover and leave to marinate in the refrigerator for 1–2 hours.

2 Heat the oil in a large frying pan, add the garlic slices and cook over a low heat, stirring, for 1 minute, or until golden brown. Increase the heat to medium-high, add the steak cubes and cook, stirring constantly, for 2–3 minutes until browned and almost cooked to your liking.

3 Add the sherry and cook until it has evaporated slightly. Season to taste with salt and turn into a warmed serving dish. Garnish with chopped parsley and serve hot, accompanied by crusty bread to mop up the juices.

CHICKEN LIVERS IN SHERRY SAUCE

Serves: 6   **Prep: 20 mins**   **Cook: 12–14 mins**

Ingredients

450 g/1 lb chicken livers

2 tbsp Spanish olive oil

1 small onion, finely chopped

2 garlic cloves, finely chopped

100 ml/3½ fl oz dry Spanish sherry

salt and pepper

2 tbsp chopped fresh flat-leaf parsley, plus extra sprigs, to garnish

crusty bread or toast, to serve

Method

1 If necessary, trim the chicken livers, cutting away any ducts and gristle, then cut them into small, bite-sized pieces. Heat the olive oil in a large, heavy-based frying pan. Add the onion and fry for 5 minutes, or until softened but not browned. Add the garlic and fry for a further 30 seconds.

2 Add the chicken livers to the pan and fry for 2–3 minutes, stirring constantly, until they are firm and have changed colour on the outside but are still pink and soft in the centre. Using a slotted spoon, lift the chicken livers from the pan, transfer them to a large, warmed serving dish or several smaller ones and keep warm.

3 Add the sherry to the frying pan, increase the heat and let it bubble for 3–4 minutes to evaporate the alcohol and reduce slightly. At the same time, deglaze the pan by scraping all the bits on the base of the pan into the sauce with a wooden spoon. Season the sauce to taste with salt and pepper.

4 Pour the sherry sauce over the chicken livers and sprinkle over the parsley. Garnish with parsley sprigs and serve piping hot with chunks or slices of crusty bread or toast to mop up the sauce.

CHICKEN ROLLS WITH OLIVES

Serves: 6-8   **Prep: 25 mins**   **Cook: 25-30 mins**

Ingredients

115 g/4 oz black Spanish olives in oil, drained and 2 tbsp oil reserved

140 g/5 oz butter, softened

4 tbsp chopped fresh parsley

4 skinless, boneless chicken breasts

Method

1 Preheat the oven to 200°C/400°F/Gas Mark 6. Stone and finely chop the olives. Mix together the olives, butter and parsley in a bowl.

2 Place the chicken breasts between two sheets of clingfilm and gently beat with a meat mallet or the side of a rolling pin.

3 Spread the olive and parsley butter over one side of each flattened chicken breast and roll up.

4 Secure with wooden cocktail sticks or tie with kitchen string.

5 Place the chicken rolls in an ovenproof dish. Drizzle over the reserved oil from the olives and bake in the preheated oven for 25–30 minutes, or until tender and the juices run clear when a skewer is inserted into the thickest part of the meat.

6 Transfer the chicken rolls to a chopping board, discard the cocktail sticks or string and slice with a sharp knife.

7 Transfer to a warmed serving plate and serve immediately.

MEAT & POULTRY DISHES

CHICKEN WINGS WITH TOMATO DRESSING

Serves: 6–8

Prep: 20 mins, plus marinating, cooling & chilling

Cook: 25–30 mins

Ingredients

175 ml/6 fl oz Spanish olive oil

3 garlic cloves, finely chopped

1 tsp ground cumin

1 kg/2 lb 4 oz chicken wings

2 tomatoes, peeled, deseeded and diced

5 tbsp white wine vinegar

1 tbsp shredded fresh basil leaves

Method

1 Preheat the oven to 180°C/350°F/Gas Mark 4. Mix 1 tablespoon of the oil with the garlic and cumin in a shallow dish. Cut off and discard the tips of the chicken wings and add the wings to the spice mixture, turning to coat. Cover with clingfilm and leave to marinate in a cool place for 15 minutes.

2 Heat 3 tablespoons of the remaining oil in a large, heavy-based frying pan. Add the chicken wings, in batches, and cook, turning frequently, until golden brown. Transfer to a roasting tin.

3 Roast the chicken wings for 10–15 minutes, or until tender and the juices run clear when the point of a sharp knife is inserted into the thickest part of the meat.

4 Meanwhile, mix the remaining olive oil, the tomatoes, vinegar and basil together in a bowl.

5 Using tongs, transfer the chicken wings to a non-metallic dish. Pour the dressing over them, turning to coat. Cover with clingfilm, leave to cool, then chill for 4 hours. Remove from the refrigerator 30–60 minutes before serving to return them to room temperature.

MEAT & POULTRY DISHES

POTATOES WITH CHORIZO

Serves: 4   **Prep: 15 mins**   **Cook: 30–35 mins**

Ingredients

1 tbsp Spanish olive oil

500 g/1 lb 2 oz potatoes, peeled and cut into chunky pieces

190 g/6½ oz chorizo, outer casing removed and thickly sliced

55 g/2 oz bacon lardons

300 ml/10 fl oz water

½ tsp sweet smoked paprika

1 garlic clove, crushed

1 bay leaf

pinch of crushed dried chillies

pepper

chopped fresh flat-leaf parsley, to garnish

Method

1 Heat the oil in a large, heavy based frying pan. Add the potatoes, and fry for 10 minutes, stirring occasionally until browned. Add the chorizo and bacon. Fry for a further 2–3 minutes until their fat begins to run.

2 Stir in the water, paprika, garlic, bay leaf and chillies. Cover the pan and simmer for 15–20 minutes, stirring several times, until the potatoes are tender. Season with pepper. Sprinkle with chopped parsley to garnish and serve.

MEAT & POULTRY DISHES

SPARE RIBS COATED IN PAPRIKA SAUCE

Serves: 6

Prep: 20–25 mins

Cook: 1 hour 10 mins

Ingredients

Spanish olive oil, for oiling

1.25 kg/2 lb 12 oz pork spare ribs

Paprika Sauce

100 ml/3½ fl oz dry Spanish sherry

5 tsp hot or sweet smoked Spanish paprika

2 garlic cloves, crushed

1 tbsp dried oregano

150 ml/5 fl oz water

salt

Method

1 Preheat the oven to 220°C/425°F/Gas Mark 7. Oil a large roasting tin. If the butcher has not already done so, cut the sheets of spare ribs into individual ribs. If possible, cut each spare rib in half widthways. Put the spare ribs in the prepared tin, in a single layer, and roast in the preheated oven for 20 minutes.

2 To make the sauce, put all the sauce ingredients in a jug and mix together well. Reduce the oven temperature to 180°C/350°F/Gas Mark 4. Pour off the fat from the tin, then pour the sauce over the spare ribs and turn the spare ribs to coat on both sides. Roast for a further 45 minutes, until tender, basting the spare ribs with the sauce once halfway through the cooking time.

3 Pile the spare ribs into a warmed serving dish. Bring the sauce in the roasting tin to the boil on the hob, then reduce the heat and simmer until reduced by half. Pour the sauce over the spare ribs and serve hot.

MEAT & POULTRY DISHES

ASPARAGUS WRAPPED IN HAM

Makes: 16   **Prep: 20 mins**   **Cook: 20–25 mins**

Ingredients

16 asparagus spears

8 thin slices Serrano ham,
cut in half lengthways

Spanish olive
oil, for brushing

salt

Aïoli, to serve

Method

1 Hold each asparagus spear at each end and
   bend until the woody stalk snaps off. Discard the
   broken ends.

2 Bring a frying pan of lightly salted water to the
   boil. Lay as many asparagus spears in the pan as
   will fit in a single layer. Bring back to the boil, then
   turn off the heat, cover and leave to steam for
   3–5 minutes, until just tender.

3 Use tongs to transfer the asparagus to a bowl of
   iced water. Repeat with any remaining spears.
   Pat the asparagus dry and wrap a piece of ham
   around each spear.

4 Heat a ridged griddle pan over a high heat.
   Lightly brush with oil. Add as many asparagus
   spears as will fit in a single layer and fry, turning
   occasionally, for 3–5 minutes, until the ham
   is crisp. Repeat until all the spears have
   been cooked.

5 Transfer to a serving platter. Serve warm or at
   room temperature with aïoli for dipping.

MEAT & POULTRY DISHES

CHORIZO IN RED WINE

Serves: 6

Prep: 15 mins,
plus marinating

Cook: 25–30 mins

Ingredients

200 g/7 oz chorizo

200 ml/7 fl oz Spanish
red wine

2 tbsp brandy

fresh flat-leaf parsley sprigs,
to garnish

crusty bread, to serve

Method

1 Use a fork to prick the chorizo a few times. Place the chorizo and wine in a large saucepan. Bring the wine to the boil, then reduce the heat, cover and simmer gently for 15–20 minutes.

2 Transfer the chorizo and wine to a bowl, cover and leave to marinate for 8 hours or overnight.

3 Drain the chorizo, reserving the wine. Remove the outer casing from the chorizo and cut the sausage into 5-mm/¼-inch slices. Place the chorizo slices in a large, heavy-based frying pan.

4 Pour the brandy into a small saucepan and heat gently.

5 Pour the brandy over the chorizo slices, stand well back and set it alight.

6 When the flames have died down, gently shake the pan, add the reserved wine and cook over a high heat until almost all of the wine has evaporated.

7 Serve piping hot, garnished with parsley sprigs and accompanied by bread.

TINY MEATBALLS IN ALMOND SAUCE

Serves: 6

Prep: 30–35 mins, plus soaking & cooling

Cook: 40–45 mins

Ingredients

55 g/2 oz white or brown bread, crusts removed

3 tbsp water

450 g/1 lb fresh lean pork mince

1 large onion, finely chopped

1 garlic clove, chopped

2 tbsp chopped fresh flat-leaf parsley, plus extra to garnish

1 egg, beaten

freshly grated nutmeg

plain flour, for coating

2 tbsp Spanish olive oil

lemon juice, to taste

salt and pepper

Almond sauce

2 tbsp Spanish olive oil

25 g/1 oz white or brown bread, broken into pieces

115 g/4 oz blanched almonds

2 garlic cloves, finely chopped

150 ml/5 fl oz dry white wine

425 ml/15 fl oz vegetable stock

salt and pepper

Method

1 Put the bread into a bowl, add the water and leave to soak for 5 minutes. Using your hands, squeeze out the water and transfer the bread to a dry bowl. Add the pork, onion, garlic, parsley and egg. Season with nutmeg, salt and pepper and knead the ingredients together well.

2 Spread some flour on a plate. Using floured hands, shape the meat mixture into about 30 equal-sized balls, then roll each meatball in flour until coated.

3 Heat the oil in a large, heavy-based frying pan. Add the meatballs, in batches if necessary, and fry for 4–5 minutes, or until brown on all sides. Using a slotted spoon, remove the meatballs from the frying pan and set aside.

4 To make the sauce, heat the oil in the same pan. Add the bread and almonds and gently fry, stirring frequently, until golden brown.

5 Add the finely chopped garlic and fry for a further 30 seconds, then pour in the wine and boil for 1–2 minutes. Season to taste with salt and pepper and leave to cool slightly.

MEAT & POULTRY DISHES

6 Transfer the bread and almond mixture to a food processor. Add the stock and process until smooth. Return to the pan.

7 Carefully add the meatballs to the sauce and simmer for 25 minutes, or until tender. Taste the sauce and season with salt and pepper if needed.

8 Transfer to a warmed serving dish, add a squeeze of lemon juice to taste and garnish with chopped parsley. Serve immediately.

CRISPY CHICKEN & HAM CROQUETTES

Makes: 8

Prep: 30 mins,
plus cooling & chilling

Cook: 22–28 mins

Ingredients

4 tbsp Spanish olive oil

4 tbsp plain flour

200 ml/7 fl oz milk

115 g/4 oz cooked chicken, minced

55 g/2 oz Serrano ham, very finely chopped

1 tbsp chopped fresh flat-leaf parsley

small pinch of freshly grated nutmeg

1 egg, beaten

55 g/2 oz day-old white breadcrumbs

sunflower oil, for deep-frying

salt and pepper

Aïoli, to serve

Method

1 Heat the olive oil in a saucepan over a medium heat. Stir in the flour to form a paste and cook gently for 1 minute, stirring constantly.

2 Remove the pan from the heat and gradually stir in the milk until smooth. Return to the heat and slowly bring to the boil, stirring constantly, until the mixture boils and begins to thicken.

3 Remove the pan from the heat, add the chicken and beat until the mixture is smooth. Add the ham, parsley and nutmeg and mix well. Season to taste with salt and pepper.

4 Spread the chicken mixture in a dish and leave for 30 minutes until cool, then cover and chill for 2–3 hours or overnight.

5 Divide the chicken mixture into eight portions. Use wet hands to form each portion into a cylindrical shape.

6 Pour the beaten egg onto a plate and put the breadcrumbs on a separate plate. Dip the croquettes, one at a time, in the beaten egg, then roll in the breadcrumbs to coat. Chill for at least 1 hour.

7 Heat enough sunflower oil for deep-frying in a large saucepan or deep-fat fryer to 180–190°C/350–375°F, or until a cube of bread browns in 30 seconds. Add the croquettes, and deep-fry for 5–10 minutes, or until golden brown and crisp.

8 Remove the croquettes with a slotted spoon and drain well on kitchen paper.

9 Serve the croquettes piping hot, accompanied by aïoli for dipping.

BEEF SKEWERS WITH ORANGE & GARLIC

Serves: 6–8

Prep: 20–25 mins, plus marinating

Cook: 10 mins

Ingredients

3 tbsp white wine

2 tbsp Spanish olive oil

3 garlic cloves, finely chopped

juice of 1 orange

450 g/1 lb rump steak, cubed

salt and pepper

450 g/1 lb baby onions, halved

2 orange peppers, deseeded and cut into squares

225 g/8 oz cherry tomatoes, halved

Method

1 Mix the wine, olive oil, garlic and orange juice together in a shallow, non-metallic dish. Add the cubes of beef, season to taste with salt and pepper and toss to coat. Cover with clingfilm and leave to marinate in the refrigerator for 2–8 hours.

2 Preheat the grill to high. Drain the beef, reserving the marinade. Thread the beef, onions, peppers and tomatoes alternately onto several small skewers.

3 Cook under the hot grill, turning and brushing frequently with the marinade, for 10 minutes, or until cooked through. Transfer to warmed serving plates and serve immediately.

LAMB SKEWERS WITH LEMON

Serves: 8

Prep: 20–25 mins, plus marinating

Cook: 10 mins

Ingredients

2 garlic cloves, finely chopped

1 Spanish onion, finely chopped

2 tsp finely grated lemon rind

2 tbsp lemon juice

1 tsp fresh thyme leaves

1 tsp ground coriander

1 tsp ground cumin

2 tbsp red wine vinegar

125 ml/4 fl oz Spanish olive oil

1 kg/2 lb 4 oz lamb fillet, cut into 2-cm/¾-inch pieces

orange or lemon slices, to garnish

Method

1 Mix the garlic, onion, lemon rind, lemon juice, thyme, coriander, cumin, vinegar and olive oil together in a large, shallow, non-metallic dish, whisking well until thoroughly combined.

2 Thread the pieces of lamb onto 16 wooden skewers and add to the dish, turning well to coat. Cover with clingfilm and leave to marinate in the refrigerator for 2–8 hours, turning occasionally.

3 Preheat the grill to medium. Drain the skewers, reserving the marinade. Cook under the hot grill, turning frequently and brushing with the marinade, for 10 minutes, or until tender and cooked to your liking.

4 Serve immediately, garnished with orange or lemon slices.

SPANISH MEATBALLS WITH CRACKED OLIVES

Serves: 6

Prep: 30–35 mins, plus soaking

Cook: 55–60 mins

Ingredients

55 g/2 oz day-old bread, crusts removed

3 tbsp water

250 g/9 oz lean fresh pork mince

250 g/9 oz lean fresh lamb mince

2 small onions, finely chopped

3 garlic cloves, crushed

1 tsp ground cumin

1 tsp ground coriander

1 egg, lightly beaten

plain flour, for dusting

3 tbsp Spanish olive oil

400 g/14 oz canned chopped tomatoes

5 tbsp dry sherry or red wine

pinch of hot or sweet smoked Spanish paprika

pinch of sugar

175 g/6 oz cracked green Spanish olives in extra virgin olive oil

salt

crusty bread, to serve

Method

1 Put the bread in a bowl, add the water and leave to soak for 5 minutes. Using your hands, squeeze out as much of the water as possible from the bread and put the bread in a clean bowl.

2 Add the mince, 1 chopped onion, 2 crushed garlic cloves, the cumin, coriander and egg to the bread. Season to taste with salt and, using your hands, mix together well. Dust a plate or baking sheet with flour. Using floured hands, roll the mixture into 30 equal-sized, small balls, put on the plate or baking sheet and roll lightly in the flour.

3 Heat 2 tablespoons of the oil in a large frying pan, add the meatballs, in batches to avoid overcrowding, and cook over a medium heat, turning frequently, for 8–10 minutes until golden brown on all sides and firm. Remove with a slotted spoon and set aside.

4 Heat the remaining oil in the frying pan, add the remaining onion and cook, stirring occasionally, for 5 minutes, or until softened but not browned. Add the remaining garlic and cook, stirring, for 30 seconds.

MEAT & POULTRY DISHES

5 Add the tomatoes, sherry, paprika and sugar and season to taste with salt. Bring to the boil, then reduce the heat and simmer for 10 minutes.

6 Using a handheld blender, blend the tomato mixture until smooth. Alternatively, turn the tomato mixture into a food processor or blender and process until smooth. Return the sauce to the frying pan.

7 Carefully return the meatballs to the frying pan and add the olives. Simmer gently for 20 minutes, or until the meatballs are tender. Serve hot, with crusty bread to mop up the sauce.

PAELLA DI MARISCO

Serves: 6

Prep: 25–30 mins

Cook: 1 hour 5 mins–1¼ hours, plus resting

Ingredients

4 tbsp extra virgin olive oil

1 kg/2 lb 4 oz chicken legs, thighs and wings, trimmed of excess fat

250 g/9 oz squid, cleaned and chopped into bite-sized rings

2 large Spanish onions, finely chopped

1 red pepper, cored, deseeded and chopped

6 garlic cloves, finely chopped

375 g/13 oz paella rice

large pinch of saffron

700 ml/1¼ pints warm chicken stock

125 ml/4 fl oz white wine

4 large ripe tomatoes, peeled and diced, or 400 g/14 oz canned chopped tomatoes

½ tsp hot smoked paprika

1 tbsp fresh thyme leaves

1 tsp salt

250 g/9 oz mussels, cockles or small clams, cleaned

250 g/9 oz large cooked prawns, shell on

250 g/9 oz frozen peas or baby broad beans, thawed

handful chopped parsley

lemon wedges and a green salad, to serve

Method

1 Add a splash of oil to a paella pan and place over a high heat. Add the chicken and turn it occasionally until brown but not cooked through then set aside. Add the squid, fry quickly and set aside. Reduce the heat to low, add the remaining oil, the onions and the red pepper and gently fry for 15–20 minutes until soft. Add the garlic and fry for a further 5 minutes. Stir the rice into the mixture and fry for 1 minute. Everything up to this point can be done in advance.

2 Add the saffron to the stock, then add the stock to the rice with the wine, tomatoes, paprika, thyme, cooked chicken, salt and mussels. Bring to the boil and simmer, uncovered, over a low heat for 20 minutes, giving the pan an occasional turn and shake (do not stir) to prevent it burning on the base.

3 Push the cooked prawns into the mixture, then scatter the peas, parsley and cooked squid on top and cook for another 10–15 minutes until the rice is cooked and the stock has almost evaporated. Discard any unopened mussels, cover with foil or a lid and leave to rest for 5 minutes before placing the pan on the table with the lemon wedges on top. Serve with a green salad.

MEAT & POULTRY DISHES

CHICKEN SALAD WITH RAISINS & PINE NUTS

Serves: 6-8

Prep: 20 mins,
plus cooling & optional chilling

Cook: 15 mins

Ingredients

50 ml/2 fl oz red wine vinegar

25 g/1 oz caster sugar

1 bay leaf

pared rind of 1 lemon

150 g/5½ oz seedless raisins

4 large skinless, boneless chicken breasts, about 600 g/1 lb 5 oz in total

5 tbsp Spanish olive oil

1 garlic clove, finely chopped

150 g/5½ oz pine kernels

salt and pepper

100 ml/3½ fl oz Spanish extra virgin olive oil

1 small bunch fresh flat-leaf parsley, finely chopped

Method

1 To make the dressing, put the vinegar, sugar, bay leaf and lemon rind in a saucepan and bring to the boil, then remove from the heat. Stir in the raisins and leave to cool.

2 When the dressing is cool, slice the chicken breasts widthways into very thin slices. Heat the olive oil in a large frying pan, add the chicken slices and cook over a medium heat, stirring occasionally, for 8–10 minutes until lightly browned and tender.

3 Add the garlic and pine kernels and cook, stirring constantly and shaking the pan, for 1 minute, or until the pine kernels are golden brown. Season to taste with salt and pepper.

4 Pour the cooled dressing into a large bowl, discarding the bay leaf and lemon rind. Add the extra virgin olive oil and whisk together. Season to taste with salt and pepper. Add the chicken mixture and parsley and toss together. Turn the salad into a serving dish and serve warm or, if serving cold, cover and chill in the refrigerator for 2–3 hours before serving.

MEAT & POULTRY DISHES

CHICKEN MORSELS FRIED IN BATTER

Serves: 6–8

Prep: 25 mins,
plus marinating

Cook: 30 mins

Ingredients

500 g/1 lb 2 oz skinless,
boneless chicken thighs

3 tbsp olive oil

juice of ½ lemon

2 garlic cloves, crushed

8 tbsp plain flour

vegetable oil for
deep-frying

2 eggs, beaten

salt and pepper

coarsely chopped fresh
flat-leaf parsley, to garnish

lemon wedges, to serve

Method

1 Cut the chicken thighs into 4-cm/1½-inch chunks. Mix the olive oil, lemon juice, garlic, salt and pepper in a bowl. Add the chicken pieces and leave to marinate at room temperature for an hour, or overnight in the refrigerator.

2 Spread the flour on a plate and mix with a pinch of salt and plenty of black pepper.

3 When ready to cook, remove the chicken pieces from the marinade and drain.

4 Heat the vegetable oil in a deep-fat fryer or large saucepan to 180–190°C/350–375°F until a cube of bread browns in 30 seconds. Roll the chicken in the seasoned flour and then in beaten egg. Immediately drop into the hot oil, a few pieces at a time, and deep-fry for about 5 minutes until golden and crisp, turning occasionally with tongs. Drain on crumpled kitchen paper.

5 Place the chicken pieces in a warm serving dish and sprinkle with parsley. Serve hot with thick wedges of lemon.

MEAT & POULTRY DISHES

MUSHROOMS STUFFED WITH SPINACH & BACON

Serves: 4 **Prep: 20 mins** **Cook: 30 mins**

Ingredients

225 g/8 oz fresh baby spinach leaves

4 portobello mushrooms

3 tbsp olive oil

55 g/2 oz rindless bacon, finely diced

2 garlic cloves, crushed

55 g/2 oz fresh white or brown breadcrumbs

2 tbsp fresh basil, chopped

salt and pepper

Method

1 Preheat the preheated oven to 200°C/400°F/ Gas Mark 6. Rinse the spinach and place in a saucepan with only the water clinging to the leaves. Cook for 2–3 minutes, until wilted. Drain, squeezing out as much liquid as possible, and chop finely.

2 Cut the stalks from the mushrooms and chop finely, reserving the whole caps.

3 Heat 2 tablespoons of the oil in a frying pan. Add the mushroom caps, rounded-side down, and fry for 1 minute. Remove from the frying pan and arrange, rounded-side down, in a large baking dish.

4 Add the chopped mushroom stalks, bacon and garlic to the frying pan and fry for 5 minutes. Stir in the spinach, breadcrumbs, basil and salt and pepper to taste. Mix well and divide the stuffing between the mushroom caps.

5 Drizzle the remaining oil over the top and bake in the oven for 20 minutes, until crisp and golden.

CHORIZO BREAD PARCELS

Makes: 16

Prep: 40–45 mins, plus rising

Cook: 20 mins

Ingredients

200 g/7 oz strong white flour, plus extra for dusting

1½ tsp easy-blend dried yeast

½ tsp salt

¼ tsp caster sugar

125 ml/4 fl oz warm water

sunflower oil, for oiling

115 g/4 oz chorizo, outer casing removed

Method

1 Put the flour, yeast, salt and sugar into a large bowl and make a well in the centre. Pour the water into the well and gradually mix in the flour from the side. Using your hands, mix together to form a soft dough that leaves the side of the bowl clean.

2 Turn out the dough onto a lightly floured work surface and knead for 10 minutes, or until smooth and elastic and no longer sticky. Shape the dough into a ball and put in a clean bowl. Cover with a clean, damp tea towel and leave in a warm place for 1 hour, or until the dough has risen and doubled in size.

3 Preheat the oven to 200°C/400°F/Gas Mark 6. Oil a baking sheet. Cut the chorizo into 16 equal-sized chunks. Turn out the risen dough onto a lightly floured work surface and knead lightly for 2–3 minutes to knock out the air. Divide into 16 equal-sized pieces. Shape each piece into a ball and roll out on a lightly floured work surface to a 12-cm/4½-inch round.

4 Put a piece of chorizo on each round, gather the dough at the top, enclosing the chorizo, and pinch the edges together to seal. Put each parcel, pinched-side down, on the prepared baking sheet.

5 Bake in the preheated oven for 20 minutes until pale golden brown. Turn the parcels over so that the pinched ends are uppermost and arrange in a serving basket. Serve hot, as soon after baking as possible.

CATALAN SAUSAGE & BEAN STEW

Serves: 6　　　　　**Prep: 20 mins**　　　　**Cook: 1 hour**

Ingredients

2 tbsp olive oil, plus extra for frying

5 rashers unsmoked bacon, derinded and cut into 1-cm/½-inch strips

2 onions, chopped

3 large garlic cloves, finely chopped

6 large pork sausages

450 g/1 lb chorizo, outer casing removed in 1 piece

400 g/14 oz canned butter beans, drained and rinsed

1 litre/1¾ pints chicken stock

250 g/9 oz fresh or frozen broad beans

6 tbsp chopped flat-leaf parsley

crusty bread, to serve

Method

1 Heat the oil in a casserole and fry the bacon over a medium-low heat for 10 minutes until starting to colour. Remove with a slotted spoon and set aside. Add the onions and gently fry for 15 minutes, stirring, until golden. Add the garlic and fry for a further 5 minutes.

2 Meanwhile, put the pork sausages in a frying pan and cook over a medium heat, in a little oil if necessary, and without pricking them, until golden but not brown. Remove from the pan and slice each sausage into four pieces. Remove the skin from the chorizo, and slice the chorizo into 2.5-cm/1-inch chunks.

3 Return the bacon to the casserole, then add both types of sausage and the butter beans. Pour in the stock, cover and bring to the boil, then reduce the heat and simmer for 15 minutes.

4 Add the broad beans and half the parsley. Return to the boil, then simmer for 5 minutes until just tender (do not overcook). Sprinkle with the remaining parsley and serve with hunks of crusty bread to mop up the juices.

SAUTÉED VEAL STRIPS WITH PEPPERS

Serves: 8

Prep: 20–25 mins, plus cooling

Cook: 25 mins

Ingredients

3 large red peppers, deseeded and quartered

3–4 tbsp olive oil

700 g/1 lb 9 oz veal (or pork) escalopes, cut into ½ inch/1 cm strips

85 g/3 oz streaky bacon, chopped

2 onions, sliced

3 garlic cloves, finely chopped

250 g/9 oz ripe red tomatoes, seeded and roughly chopped

125 ml/4 fl oz Amontillado or cream sherry

chopped fresh flat leaf parsley, to garnish

Method

1 Preheat the grill to high. Arrange the peppers skin-side up on a grill pan. Grill close to the heat for 4 minutes until the skin blackens and blisters. Transfer to a polythene bag and leave to cool. Peel off the skin and cut into strips.

2 Heat 1 tablespoon of the oil in a large heavy-based frying pan set over a medium-high heat. Fry the veal in several batches for 2 minutes, stirring until lightly browned and adding a little extra oil as necessary. Transfer to a plate with a slotted spoon.

3 Add the bacon to the pan and heat until the fat runs, then add the onions and garlic and cook over a low heat until softened. Add the tomatoes and sherry. Continue cooking for a further 5 minutes until the tomatoes are pulpy and most of the liquid has evaporated.

4 Return the veal and any juices to the pan with the peppers. Heat through for 1–2 minutes. Sprinkle with chopped parsley to garnish and serve immediately.

★ **Variation**

If you prefer, play it safer with pork or chicken instead of veal.

MEAT & POULTRY DISHES

FISH & OTHER SEAFOOD

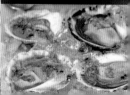

TRADITIONAL CATALAN SALT COD SALAD

Serves: 4–6

Prep: 30–35 mins, plus soaking & marinating

Cook: 6–8 mins

Ingredients

400 g/14 oz dried salt cod in one piece

6 spring onions, thinly sliced on the diagonal

6 tbsp extra virgin olive oil

1 tbsp sherry vinegar

1 tbsp lemon juice

2 large red peppers, grilled, peeled, deseeded and very finely diced

12 large black olives, stoned and sliced

2 large, juicy tomatoes, thinly sliced, to serve

2 tbsp very finely chopped fresh parsley, to garnish

pepper

Method

1 Place the dried salt cod in a large bowl, cover with cold water and leave to soak for at least 48 hours, changing the water occasionally.

2 Pat the salt cod very dry with kitchen paper and remove the skin and bones, then use your fingers to tear into fine shreds. Put in a large, non-metallic bowl with the spring onions, oil, vinegar and lemon juice and toss together. Season with freshly ground black pepper, cover and put in the refrigerator to marinate for 3 hours.

3 Stir in the peppers and olives. Taste and adjust the seasoning, if necessary, remembering that the cod and olives might be salty. Arrange the tomato slices on a large platter or individual plates and spoon the salad on top. Sprinkle with parsley and serve.

★ **Variation**

Garnish the dish with 2–3 hard-boiled eggs, quartered.

ANCHOVIES WITH CHORIZO & FENNEL

Serves: 8   **Prep: 25–30 mins**   **Cook: 24–34 mins**

Ingredients

100 g/3½ oz chorizo

1 fennel bulb, trimmed and very finely chopped

2 tsp fennel seeds

pinch of dried chilli flakes, or to taste

4 large tomatoes, peeled, deseeded and roughly chopped

Spanish olive oil, for brushing

8 fresh anchovies, heads removed and gutted

salt and pepper

lemon wedges, to serve

Method

1 Remove and discard the casing from the chorizo, then chop.

2 Add the chorizo to a large, dry frying pan over a high heat and fry, stirring, for 3–5 minutes, until it gives off its fat.

3 Add the fennel, reduce the heat to medium and fry, stirring, for 5–8 minutes, until soft.

4 Add the fennel seeds and chilli flakes and stir for a further minute.

5 Add the tomatoes and season to taste with salt and pepper.

6 Simmer for 15–20 minutes, stirring occasionally, until the tomatoes break down and a sauce forms.

7 Meanwhile, preheat the grill to high. Brush the grill pan with oil. Add the anchovies, sprinkle with salt and grill on each side for 2 minutes, or until cooked through and tender.

8 Transfer the anchovies to a chopping board and cut each one into two fillets, removing the bone.

9 Divide the sauce between eight small bowls and arrange two anchovy fillets on top of each. Serve with lemon wedges for squeezing over.

DEEP-FRIED WHITEBAIT

Serves: 4   **Prep: 25 mins**   **Cook: 20 mins**

Ingredients

450 g/1 lb fresh whitebait

100 g/3½ oz plain flour

50 g/1¾ oz cornflour

½ tsp salt

200 ml/7 fl oz cold water

1 egg

a few ice cubes

vegetable oil,
for deep-frying

Aïoli, to serve

Method

1 Rinse the whitebait and pat dry. Place on kitchen paper and set aside until needed.

2 Sift together the flour, cornflour and salt into a shallow dish.

3 Whisk together the water, egg and ice cubes in a jug, then pour onto the flour mixture. Whisk briefly until the mixture is runny, but still lumpy with dry bits of flour still apparent.

4 Meanwhile, heat enough oil for deep-frying in a large saucepan or deep-fat fryer to 180–190°C/350–375°F, or until a cube of bread browns in 30 seconds.

5 Dip the whitebait, a few at a time, into the batter and carefully drop into the hot oil.

6 Deep-fry for 1 minute, until the batter is crisp but not brown. Drain on kitchen paper and keep warm while you cook the remaining whitebait.

7 Serve the whitebait hot with aïoli.

SEAFOOD CROQUETTES

Makes: 24

Prep: 35 mins,
plus cooling & chilling

Cook: 30 mins

Ingredients

5 tbsp Spanish olive oil, plus extra for deep-frying

70 g/2½ oz plain flour

400 ml/14 fl oz milk

225 g/8 oz prepared cooked seafood, such as cod, hake, clams, prawns, salmon and salt cod, any skin and bones removed, very finely chopped

finely grated rind of 1 lemon

75 g/2¾ oz fine dry white breadcrumbs

1 large egg, beaten with 1 tbsp water

salt and pepper

Method

1 Heat the olive oil in a saucepan over a medium heat. Gradually stir in the flour and continue stirring for 2 minutes.

2 Remove from the heat and gradually stir in the milk, stirring constantly to prevent lumps forming. Return the pan to the heat and bring to the boil, stirring until the sauce is smooth and thick.

3 Stir in the seafood and lemon rind and season to taste with salt and pepper. Transfer to a bowl and leave to cool. Cover the surface with clingfilm and chill for at least 4 hours or overnight.

4 Use wet hands to divide the seafood mixture into 24 balls. Wet your hands again, then roll the balls into 5 cm/2 inch long cork shapes.

5 Put the breadcrumbs into a shallow bowl. One by one, dip the croquettes in the egg mixture and then roll in the breadcrumbs until coated.

6 Heat enough oil for deep-frying in a saucepan or deep-fat fryer to 180–190°C/350–375°F, or until a cube of bread browns in 30 seconds. Add the croquettes to the pan, in batches, and fry for 2–2½ minutes, until golden brown.

7 Transfer to a plate lined with kitchen paper and keep in a warm oven until all the croquettes are cooked. Serve hot.

MONKFISH BITES WITH MOJO VERDE SAUCE

Serves: 8

Prep: 25 mins,
plus chilling

Cook: 15–20 mins

Ingredients

900 g/2 lb skinless, boneless
monkfish fillets

2 tbsp Spanish olive oil

Mojo verde sauce

1 large garlic clove,
chopped

1 fresh green chilli,
deseeded and chopped

1 green pepper, deseeded
and chopped

30 g/1 oz fresh
coriander leaves

125 ml/4 fl oz Spanish extra
virgin olive oil

1 tbsp sherry vinegar,
or to taste

salt and pepper

Method

1 To make the sauce, put the garlic, chilli, green pepper and coriander into a food processor and blend until a paste forms.

2 Add the extra virgin olive oil and vinegar and blend until smooth. Season to taste with salt and pepper. Chill for up to 1 hour.

3 Using a small knife, remove the thin, grey membrane from the monkfish.

4 Cut the monkfish into bite-sized pieces.

5 Heat the olive oil in a large frying pan over a medium heat. Working in batches, fry the monkfish pieces, turning once, for 3–5 minutes, until just cooked through.

6 Drain well on kitchen paper. Transfer the pieces of fish to a plate and spear with wooden cocktail sticks.

7 Serve immediately with the sauce for dipping.

CLAMS WITH SAFFRON & LEMON DRESSING

Serves: 8

Prep: 25 mins, plus soaking

Cook: 13–17 mins

Ingredients

2 tbsp lemon juice

1 tsp honey

finely grated rind of 1 lemon

large pinch of saffron threads, soaked for 30 minutes in 2 tsp boiling water

4 tbsp Spanish extra virgin olive oil

1 kg/2 lb 4 oz live clams, rinsed

2 tbsp Spanish olive oil

1 onion, finely chopped

2 garlic cloves, finely chopped

125 ml/4 fl oz dry white wine

salt and pepper

slices of bread from a long, thin loaf, to serve

Method

1 Add the lemon juice, honey, lemon rind, and salt and pepper to taste to the infused saffron threads. Whisk in the extra virgin olive oil.

2 Discard any clams with broken shells and any that refuse to close when tapped.

3 Heat the olive oil in a large saucepan over a medium heat. Add the onion and garlic and fry for 3–5 minutes, until soft. Add the clams and wine, cover the pan and cook, shaking the pan, for 3–5 minutes, until the clams have opened. Discard any clams that remain closed. Strain the clams, reserving the cooking liquid.

4 Return the cooking liquid to the pan and add the saffron mixture. Bring to the boil and boil until reduced by half.

5 Transfer the clams to a serving dish and pour over the saffron and lemon dressing. Serve immediately with plenty of bread.

FISH & OTHER SEAFOOD

SCALLOP & SERRANO HAM SKEWERS

Serves: 4

Prep: 20–25 mins, plus marinating

Cook: 5 mins

Ingredients

2 tbsp lemon juice

3 tbsp Spanish olive oil

2 garlic cloves, finely chopped

1 tbsp chopped fresh parsley

12 shelled scallops, with corals

8 wafer-thin slices Serrano ham

pepper

Method

1 Mix the lemon juice, oil, garlic and parsley in a shallow, non-metallic dish.

2 Separate the corals from the scallops and add both to the dish, turning to coat. Cover with clingfilm and leave to marinate at room temperature for 20 minutes.

3 Preheat the grill to medium. Drain the scallops. Thread a scallop and a coral onto a metal skewer. Scrunch up a slice of ham and thread it onto the skewer, followed by another scallop and a coral. Repeat to fill four skewers, each with three scallops and two slices of ham.

4 Cook the skewers under the preheated grill, turning frequently, for 5 minutes, or until the scallops are tender and the ham is crisp.

5 Transfer to warmed serving plates, sprinkle with pepper and serve immediately.

FISH & OTHER SEAFOOD

MONKFISH ESCABECHE

Serves: 4

Prep: 20–25 mins, plus cooling & chilling

Cook: 30–40 mins

Ingredients

250 ml/9 fl oz Spanish extra virgin olive oil

1 large onion, thinly sliced

2 carrots, thinly sliced

4 large garlic cloves, thinly sliced

3 bay leaves

1–2 fresh green chillies, to taste, deseeded and thinly sliced

1 tbsp coriander seeds, crushed

250 ml/9 fl oz red wine vinegar or sherry vinegar

125 ml/4 fl oz dry white wine

750 g/1 lb 10 oz monkfish fillets

salt and pepper

chopped fresh coriander, to garnish

Method

1 Heat 125 ml/4 fl oz of the oil in a saucepan over a medium heat. Add the onion and carrots and fry, stirring, for 8–10 minutes, until the vegetables are very tender but not brown.

2 Add the garlic, bay leaves, chillies and coriander seeds and stir for 2 minutes. Season to taste with salt and pepper.

3 Stir in the vinegar and wine and bring to the boil, then simmer for 10 minutes. Cover and keep warm.

4 Meanwhile, using a small knife, remove the thin, grey membrane from the monkfish.

5 Cut the monkfish into bite-sized pieces.

6 Heat half the remaining oil in a large frying pan over a medium heat. Fry half the monkfish pieces, turning once, for 3–5 minutes. Repeat until all the monkfish has been cooked.

7 Drain well on kitchen paper and transfer to a non-metallic dish.

8 Pour the warm vegetable mixture and the oil left in the pan over the fish. Leave to cool completely, then cover and chill for at least 36 hours and up to five days.

9 Sprinkle with chopped coriander and serve chilled or at room temperature.

FISH & OTHER SEAFOOD

CALAMARI WITH PRAWNS & BROAD BEANS

Serves: 4–6   **Prep: 20–25 mins**   **Cook: 16–23 mins**

Ingredients

2 tbsp Spanish olive oil

4 spring onions, thinly sliced

2 garlic cloves, finely chopped

500 g/1 lb 2 oz cleaned squid bodies, thickly sliced

100 ml/3½ fl oz dry white wine

600 g/1 lb 5 oz fresh young broad beans in their pods, shelled to give about 225 g/ 8 oz, or 225 g/8 oz frozen baby broad beans

250 g/9 oz raw tiger prawns, peeled and deveined

4 tbsp chopped fresh flat-leaf parsley

salt and pepper

crusty bread, to serve

Method

1 Heat the oil in a large frying pan with a lid or a flameproof casserole, add the spring onions and cook over a medium heat, stirring occasionally, for 4–5 minutes until softened. Add the garlic and cook, stirring, for 30 seconds until softened. Add the squid slices and cook over a high heat, stirring occasionally, for 2 minutes, or until golden brown.

2 Add the wine and bring to the boil. Add the broad beans, then reduce the heat, cover and simmer for 5–8 minutes if using fresh beans or 4–5 minutes if using frozen beans, until the beans are tender.

3 Add the prawns and parsley, re-cover and simmer for a further 2–3 minutes until the prawns turn pink and start to curl. Season to taste with salt and pepper. Serve hot, with crusty bread to mop up the juices.

TUNA WITH PIMIENTO-STUFFED OLIVES

Serves: 4

Prep: 25 mins, plus marinating

Cook: 10–18 mins

Ingredients

2 fresh tuna steaks, weighing about 250 g/ 9 oz in total and about 2.5 cm/1 inch thick

5 tbsp Spanish extra virgin olive oil

3 tbsp red wine vinegar

bunch of fresh thyme sprigs

1 bay leaf

2 tbsp plain flour

1 onion, finely chopped

2 garlic cloves, finely chopped

85 g/3 oz pimiento-stuffed green olives, halved

salt and pepper

Method

1 Cut the tuna steaks in half.

2 Cut each half into 1 cm/½ inch thick slices against the grain.

3 Put 3 tablespoons of the oil and all the vinegar into a shallow, non-metallic dish. Strip the leaves from half the thyme sprigs and add to the dish with the bay leaf. Season with salt and pepper.

4 Add the tuna strips to the dish, turning to coat. Leave to marinate in the refrigerator for 8 hours or overnight.

5 Put the flour into a polythene bag. Remove the tuna strips from the marinade, reserving the marinade, and add them to the flour. Toss well until lightly coated.

6 Heat the remaining oil in a large frying pan. Add the onion and garlic and gently fry for 5–10 minutes, or until soft and golden brown.

7 Add the tuna strips to the pan and fry for 2–5 minutes, turning until the fish looks opaque.

8 Add the reserved marinade and the olives to the pan. Bring to the boil and cook for a further 1–2 minutes, stirring, until the fish is tender and the sauce has thickened.

9 Serve hot, garnished with the remaining thyme.

SEARED TUNA WITH WHITE BEANS & ARTICHOKES

Serves: 6

Prep: 25 mins, plus soaking, marinating, standing & cooling

Cook: 55 mins

Ingredients

150 ml/5 fl oz extra virgin olive oil

juice of 1 lemon

½ tsp dried chilli flakes

¼ tsp coarsely ground black pepper

4 thin fresh tuna steaks, weighing about 450 g/1 lb

225 g/8 oz dried cannellini beans, soaked overnight

1 shallot, finely chopped

1 garlic clove, crushed

2 tsp finely chopped rosemary

2 tbsp chopped flat-leaf parsley

4 oil-cured artichokes, quartered

4 vine-ripened tomatoes, sliced lengthways into segments

16 black olives, pitted

salt and pepper

lemon wedges, to serve

Method

1 Put 4 tablespoons of the olive oil in a shallow dish with 3 tablespoons of the lemon juice, the chilli flakes and black pepper. Add the tuna steaks and leave to marinate at room temperature for 1 hour, turning occasionally.

2 Meanwhile, drain the beans and put in a saucepan with plenty of fresh water to cover. Bring to the boil, then boil rapidly for 15 minutes. Reduce the heat slightly and cook for another 30 minutes, or until tender but not disintegrating. Add salt in the last 5 minutes of cooking.

3 Drain the beans and tip into a bowl. While still warm, toss with 5 tablespoons of the olive oil, then stir in the shallot, garlic, rosemary, parsley and remaining lemon juice. Season with salt and pepper to taste. Leave to stand for at least 30 minutes to allow the flavours to develop.

4 Heat the remaining tablespoon of oil in a pan until very hot. Add the tuna and the marinade, and sear for 1–2 minutes each side. Remove from the pan and allow to cool a little.

5 Tip the beans into a serving dish. Mix in the artichokes, tomatoes and olives, adding more oil and seasoning if necessary. Flake the tuna and arrange on top. Garnish with lemon wedges and serve at room temperature.

OYSTERS WITH SHERRY VINEGAR

Serves: 6

Prep: 25–30 mins, plus standing

Cook: N/A

Ingredients

1 shallot, finely chopped
3 tbsp sherry vinegar
3 tbsp red wine vinegar
1 tbsp sugar
pepper
24 fresh oysters
rock salt or crushed ice,
to serve (optional)

Method

1 Mix the shallot, vinegars and sugar together in a non-metallic bowl and season well with pepper. Cover with clingfilm and leave to stand at room temperature for at least 15 minutes to allow the flavours to mingle.

2 Meanwhile, shuck the oysters. Wrap a tea towel around your hand to protect it and hold an oyster firmly. Insert an oyster knife or other strong, sharp knife into the hinged edge and twist to prise the shells apart. Still holding both shells firmly in the wrapped hand, slide the blade of the knife along the upper shell to sever the muscle. Lift off the upper shell, being careful not to spill the liquid inside. Slide the blade of the knife along the lower shell underneath the oyster to sever the second muscle. Arrange the oysters on their half-shells in a single layer on a bed of rock salt or crushed ice, if you like.

3 Spoon the dressing evenly over the oysters and serve at room temperature.

FISH & OTHER SEAFOOD

SEARED SQUID & GOLDEN POTATOES

Serves: 8 **Prep: 20 mins** **Cook: 50 mins**

Ingredients

kg/2 lb 4 oz new potatoes

4–6 tbsp Spanish olive oil

1 large onion, thinly sliced

2 garlic cloves,
finely chopped

kg/2 lb 4 oz cleaned squid
bodies, thinly sliced

6 tbsp dry white wine

small bunch fresh flat-leaf
parsley, finely chopped

salt and pepper

lemon wedges, to serve

Method

1 Put the potatoes in a saucepan of water and bring to the boil. Reduce the heat and simmer for 20 minutes, or until tender. Drain well.

2 Heat 4 tablespoons of oil in a large flameproof casserole, add the potatoes and cook over a medium heat, stirring occasionally, for 10 minutes, or until beginning to brown. Add the onion and cook, stirring occasionally, for 10 minutes until golden brown. Add the garlic and cook, stirring, for 30 seconds until softened. Push all the ingredients to the side of the casserole.

3 If necessary, add the remaining oil to the casserole. Add the squid slices and cook over a high heat, stirring occasionally, for 2 minutes, or until golden brown. Add the wine and cook for a further 1–2 minutes. Add most of the parsley, reserving a little to garnish, and mix the potatoes, onions and garlic with the squid. Season to taste with salt and pepper.

4 Serve hot, in the casserole, sprinkled with the reserved parsley to garnish and with lemon wedges for squeezing over.

FISH & OTHER SEAFOOD

TUNA-STUFFED PEPPER STRIPS

Serves: 6

Prep: 30–35 mins,   **Cook: 40 mins**
plus cooling & chilling

Ingredients

6 mixed red, green, yellow
or orange peppers

2 tbsp Spanish olive oil

200 g/7 oz canned tuna in
olive oil, drained

100 g/3½ oz curd cheese

4 tbsp chopped fresh
flat-leaf parsley

1 garlic clove, crushed

salt and pepper

Method

1 Preheat the oven to 200°C/400°F/Gas Mark
6. Brush the peppers with the oil and put in a
roasting tin. Roast in the preheated oven for
30 minutes, turn over and roast for a further
10 minutes until the skins have blistered and
blackened.

2 Using a slotted spoon, transfer the roasted
peppers to a polythene bag and leave to
cool for about 15 minutes, or until cool enough
to handle.

3 Meanwhile, put the tuna on kitchen paper and
pat dry to remove the oil. Transfer to a food
processor, add the curd cheese, parsley and
garlic and process until mixed together. Season
to taste with salt and pepper. Using a sharp knife
or your fingers, carefully peel away the skins
from the cooled peppers. Cut the peppers into
quarters and remove the stems, cores and seeds

4 Put a heaped teaspoonful of the tuna and
cheese mixture on the pointed end of each
pepper quarter and roll up. If necessary, wipe
with kitchen paper to remove any filling that
has spread over the outsides of the rolls, then
arrange the rolls in a shallow dish with the filling
end facing up. Cover and chill in the refrigerator
for at least 2 hours until firm before serving.

FISH & OTHER SEAFOOD

ANCHOVIES WITH CELERY & ROCKET

Serves: 4

Prep: 20 mins,
plus soaking

Cook: N/A

Ingredients

2 celery sticks,
strings removed

4 small handfuls of rocket

2–16 brine-cured anchovy
fillets, halved lengthways

1½ tbsp extra virgin
olive oil

salt and pepper

thick lemon wedges,
to serve

Method

1 Quarter the celery sticks lengthways and slice into 7.5-cm/3-inch batons. Soak in ice-cold water for 30 minutes, until crisp and slightly curled, then drain and pat dry.

2 Place a small pile of rocket on individual serving plates. Arrange the celery and anchovy fillets attractively on top. Spoon over a little olive oil and season with salt and pepper, bearing in mind the saltiness of the anchovies. Serve with thick wedges of lemon.

FISH & OTHER SEAFOOD

SAFFRON PRAWNS WITH LEMON MAYONNAISE

Serves: 6-8

Prep: 40-45 mins, plus chilling & standing

Cook: 18-22 mins

Ingredients

1.25 kg/2 lb 12 oz raw jumbo prawns

85 g/3 oz plain flour

125 ml/4 fl oz light beer

2 tbsp Spanish olive oil

pinch of saffron powder

2 egg whites

vegetable oil, for deep-frying

Lemon mayonnaise

4 garlic cloves

sea salt and pepper

2 egg yolks

1 tbsp lemon juice

1 tbsp finely grated lemon rind

300 ml/10 fl oz sunflower oil

Method

1 First make the mayonnaise. Place the garlic cloves on a chopping board and sprinkle with a little sea salt, then flatten them with the side of a heavy knife. Finely chop and flatten again.

2 Transfer the garlic to a food processor or blender and add the egg yolks, lemon juice and lemon rind. Process briefly until just blended. With the motor still running, gradually add the sunflower oil through the feeder tube until it is fully incorporated. Scrape the mayonnaise into a serving bowl, season to taste with salt and pepper, then cover and leave to chill until ready to serve.

3 Pull the heads off the prawns and peel, leaving the tails intact. Cut along the length of the back of each prawn and remove and discard the dark vein. Rinse under cold running water and pat dry with kitchen paper.

4 Sift the flour into a bowl. Mix the beer, oil and saffron together in a jug, then gradually whisk into the flour. Cover and leave at room temperature for 30 minutes to rest.

5 Whisk the egg whites in a spotlessly clean, grease-free bowl until stiff. Gently fold the egg whites into the flour mixture.

Heat the vegetable oil in a deep-fat fryer or large saucepan to 180–190°C/350–375°F, or until a cube of bread browns in 30 seconds. Holding the prawns by their tails, dip them into the batter and shake off any excess. Add the prawns to the oil and deep-fry for 2–3 minutes, or until crisp. Remove with a slotted spoon and drain well on kitchen paper. Serve immediately with the mayonnaise.

MIXED SEAFOOD KEBABS WITH A CHILLI & LIME GLAZE

Makes: 8

Prep: 35 mins, plus marinating & soaking

Cook: 6–8 mins

Ingredients

16 raw tiger prawns, in their shells

350 g/12 oz monkfish or hake fillet

350 g/12 oz salmon fillet, skinned

2.5-cm/1-inch piece fresh root ginger

4 tbsp sweet chilli sauce

grated rind and juice of 1 lime

sunflower or Spanish olive oil, for oiling (optional)

lime wedges, to serve

Method

1 Pull off the heads of the prawns. With your fingers, peel away the shells, leaving the tails intact. Using a sharp knife, make a shallow slit along the length of the back of each prawn, then use the tip of the knife to lift out the dark vein and discard. Rinse the prawns under cold running water and pat dry with kitchen paper. Cut the monkfish and salmon into 2.5-cm/1-inch pieces.

2 Grate the ginger into a sieve set over a large, non-metallic bowl to catch the juice. Squeeze the grated ginger to extract all the juice and discard the pulp.

3 Add the chilli sauce and lime rind and juice to the ginger juice and mix together. Add the prepared seafood and stir to coat in the marinade. Cover and leave to marinate in the refrigerator for 30 minutes.

4 Meanwhile, if using wooden skewers, soak 8 in cold water for about 30 minutes to help prevent them from burning and the food sticking to them during cooking. If using metal skewers, lightly brush with oil.

5 Preheat the grill to high and line the grill pan with foil. Remove the seafood from the marinade,

FISH & OTHER SEAFOOD

reserving the remaining marinade, and thread an equal quantity onto each prepared skewer, leaving a little space between each piece. Arrange in the grill pan.

6 Cook the skewers under the grill, turning once and brushing with the reserved marinade, for 6–8 minutes until cooked through. Serve hot, drizzled with the marinade in the grill pan and with lime wedges for squeezing over.

ROSEMARY SKEWERS WITH MONKFISH & BACON

Serves: 12

Prep: 30–35 mins, plus marinating

Cook: 10 mins

Ingredients

350 g/12 oz monkfish tail or 250 g/9 oz monkfish fillet

12 fresh rosemary stalks

3 tbsp Spanish olive oil

juice of ½ small lemon

1 garlic clove, crushed

salt and pepper

6 thick back bacon rashers

lemon wedges, to garnish

Aïoli, to serve

Method

1 If using monkfish tail, cut either side of the central bone with a sharp knife and remove the flesh to form 2 fillets. Slice the fillets in half lengthways, then cut each fillet into 12 bite-sized chunks to give a total of 24 pieces. Place the monkfish pieces in a large bowl.

2 To prepare the rosemary skewers, strip the leaves off the stalks and reserve them, leaving a few leaves at one end. For the marinade, finely chop the reserved leaves and whisk together in a bowl with the olive oil, lemon juice, garlic and salt and pepper to taste. Add the monkfish pieces and toss until coated in the marinade. Cover and leave to marinate in the refrigerator for 1–2 hours.

3 Cut each bacon rasher in half lengthways, then in half widthways, and roll up each piece. Thread 2 pieces of monkfish alternately with 2 bacon rolls onto each of the prepared rosemary skewers.

4 Preheat the grill, griddle or barbecue. Grill the monkfish and bacon skewers for 10 minutes, turning occasionally and basting with any remaining marinade, or until cooked. Serve hot, garnished with lemon wedges for squeezing over the monkfish skewers and accompanied by a small bowl of aïoli in which to dip them.

SARDINES WITH ROMESCO SAUCE

Serves: 6

Prep: 45–50 mins, plus cooling

Cook: 55 mins–1 hour 5 mins

Ingredients

24 fresh sardines, scaled, cleaned and heads removed

115 g/4 oz plain flour

4 eggs, lightly beaten

250 g/9 oz fresh white breadcrumbs

6 tbsp chopped fresh parsley

4 tbsp chopped fresh marjoram

vegetable oil, for deep-frying

Romesco sauce

1 red pepper, halved and deseeded

2 tomatoes, halved

4 garlic cloves

125 ml/4 fl oz Spanish olive oil

1 slice white bread, diced

4 tbsp blanched almonds

1 fresh red chilli, deseeded and chopped

2 shallots, chopped

1 tsp paprika

2 tbsp red wine vinegar

2 tsp sugar

1 tbsp water

Method

1. First make the sauce. Preheat the oven to 220°C/425°F/Gas Mark 7. Place the pepper, tomatoes and garlic in an ovenproof dish and drizzle over 1 tablespoon of the olive oil, turning to coat. Bake in the preheated oven for 20–25 minutes, then remove from the oven and cool. Peel off the skins and place the flesh in a food processor.

2. Heat 1 tablespoon of the remaining oil in a frying pan. Add the bread and almonds and cook over a low heat for a few minutes, or until browned. Remove and drain on kitchen paper. Add the chilli, shallots and paprika to the pan and cook for a further 5 minutes, or until the shallots are softened.

3. Transfer the almond mixture and the shallot mixture to a food processor and add the vinegar, sugar and water. Process to a paste. With the motor still running, gradually add the remaining oil through the feeder tube. Transfer to a bowl, cover and reserve.

4. Place the sardines, skin-side up, on a chopping board and press along the length of the spines with your thumbs. Turn over and remove and

discard the bones. Place the flour and eggs in separate bowls. Mix the breadcrumbs and herbs together in a third bowl. Toss the fish in the flour, the eggs, then in the breadcrumbs.

5 Heat the vegetable oil in a large saucepan to 180–190°C/350–375°F, or until a cube of bread browns in 30 seconds. Deep-fry the fish for 4–5 minutes, or until golden and tender. Drain on kitchen paper and serve with the sauce.

COD & CAPER CROQUETTES

Makes: 12

Prep: 35–40 mins, plus cooling & chilling

Cook: 40–45 mins

Ingredients

350 g/12 oz white fish fillets, such as cod, haddock or monkfish

300 ml/10 fl oz milk

4 tbsp olive oil or 55 g/2 oz butter

55 g/2 oz plain flour

4 tbsp capers, roughly chopped

1 tsp paprika

1 garlic clove, crushed

1 tsp lemon juice

3 tbsp chopped fresh flat-leaf parsley, plus extra sprigs to garnish

1 egg, beaten

55 g/2 oz fresh white breadcrumbs

1 tbsp sesame seeds

sunflower oil, for deep-frying

salt and pepper

lemon wedges, to garnish

mayonnaise, to serve

Method

1 Place the fish in a large frying pan. Pour in the milk and season to taste. Bring to the boil, then reduce the heat, cover and simmer for 8–10 minutes, or until the fish flakes easily. Using a fish slice, remove the fish from the pan. Pour the milk into a jug and reserve. Flake the fish, removing and discarding the skin and bones.

2 Heat the olive oil or butter in a saucepan. Stir in the flour to form a paste and cook gently, stirring, for 1 minute. Remove from the heat and gradually stir in the reserved milk until smooth. Return to the heat and slowly bring to the boil, stirring, until the mixture thickens.

3 Remove from the heat, add the fish and beat until smooth. Add the capers, paprika, garlic, lemon juice and parsley and mix. Season to taste. Spread the fish mixture in a dish and leave until cool, then cover and chill for 2–3 hours or overnight.

4 When the fish mixture has chilled, pour the beaten egg onto a plate. Place the breadcrumbs and sesame seeds on a separate plate, mix together and spread out. Divide the fish mixture into 12 portions. Then, with lightly

floured hands, form each portion into a sausage shape, 7.5 cm/3 inches in length. Dip the croquettes, one at a time, in the beaten egg and roll in the breadcrumb mixture. Place on a plate and chill for 1 hour.

5 Heat the sunflower oil in a deep-fat fryer to 180–190°C/350–375°F, or until a cube of bread browns in 30 seconds. Add the croquettes, in batches, and deep-fry for 3 minutes, or until golden and crispy. Remove with a slotted spoon and drain on kitchen paper. Serve hot, garnished with lemon wedges and parsley sprigs, with mayonnaise for dipping.

MARINATED SARDINE FILLETS WITH OREGANO & FENNEL

Serves: 6

Prep: 30 mins, plus cooling & marinating

Cook: 20–25 mins

Ingredients

8 large fresh sardines, gutted and scaled

6 tbsp extra virgin olive oil

1 tbsp white wine vinegar

1 tbsp dried oregano

2 garlic cloves, crushed

1 tsp black peppercorns, crushed

½ tsp sea salt

¼ tsp dried chilli flakes

½ red onion, sliced thinly

1 fennel bulb, trimmed, quartered lengthways and sliced thinly

4 tomatoes, deseeded and sliced into thin segments

2 tbsp shredded fresh basil

Method

1 Preheat the oven to 180°C/350°F/Gas Mark 4. Place the sardines in an ovenproof baking dish. Combine the oil, vinegar, oregano and garlic, and season with the crushed pepper, sea salt and chilli flakes. Pour the mixture over the sardines. Bake for 20–25 minutes until the flesh is no longer translucent around the backbone.

2 Remove the sardines from the oven and leave to cool in the baking dish. Sprinkle with the red onion slices, cover with clingfilm and leave to marinate in the refrigerator for up to 3 days. Remove from the refrigerator 1–2 hours before serving.

3 Arrange the fennel and tomato segments on top of the sardines, spooning over some of the oily juices from the dish. Sprinkle with the basil just before serving.

SWEET PEPPERS STUFFED WITH CRAB SALAD

Serves: 4–6

Prep: 30 mins, plus cooling

Cook: 40 mins

Ingredients

1 red pepper

1 tsp Spanish olive oil

240 g/8½ oz canned crabmeat, drained and squeezed dry

1½ tbsp lemon juice, or to taste

200 g/7 oz cream cheese

16 pimientos del piquillo, drained

salt and pepper

chopped fresh parsley, to garnish

Method

1 Preheat the oven to 200°C/400°F/Gas Mark 6. Brush the red pepper with the oil and put in a roasting tin.

2 Roast the red pepper in the preheated oven for 30 minutes, turn over and roast for a further 10 minutes, until the skin has blistered and blackened.

3 Using a slotted spoon, transfer the roasted pepper to a polythene bag and leave for 15 minutes, or until cool enough to handle.

4 Peel, core and deseed the pepper.

5 Put half the crabmeat in a food processor with the red pepper flesh, lemon juice, and salt and pepper to taste. Process until well blended, then transfer to a bowl.

6 Stir in the cream cheese and the remaining crabmeat. Taste and add extra lemon juice, if needed.

7 Pat the pimientos with kitchen paper to dry and scoop out any seeds that remain in the tips.

8 Use a spoon to divide the crab salad equally among the peppers, stuffing them generously.

9 Arrange on a large serving dish. Sprinkle with chopped parsley and serve.

FISH & OTHER SEAFOOD

MIXED SEAFOOD SALAD

Serves: 4–6

Prep: 15–20 mins, plus standing

Cook: N/A

Ingredients

2 garlic cloves, crushed

juice of 1½ lemons

4 tbsp extra virgin olive oil

2 tbsp chopped fresh
flat-leaf parsley

600 g/1 lb 5 oz cooked
seafood cocktail (prawns,
mussels, clams, calamari
rings, cockles)

1 oil-cured roasted red
pepper, sliced into thin strips

12 black olives, pitted

2 tbsp shredded fresh basil

salt and pepper

Method

1 Whisk the garlic, lemon juice, olive oil and parsley with salt and pepper to taste.

2 Drain the seafood if necessary, and tip into a serving dish. Add the red pepper and olives, then mix with the garlic mixture, turning to coat. Leave in a cool place for 30 minutes to allow the flavours to develop.

3 Stir again before serving, check the seasoning and sprinkle with the basil.

BAKED SCALLOPS

Serves: 6   **Prep: 15–20 mins**   **Cook: 15–20 mins**

Ingredients

700 g/1 lb 9 oz shelled scallops, chopped

2 onions, finely chopped

2 garlic cloves, finely chopped

3 tbsp chopped fresh parsley

pinch of freshly grated nutmeg

pinch of ground cloves

2 tbsp fresh white breadcrumbs

2 tbsp olive oil

salt and pepper

Method

1 Preheat the oven to 200°C/400°F/Gas Mark 6. Mix the scallops, onions, garlic, 2 tablespoons of the parsley, the nutmeg and cloves together in a bowl and season to taste with salt and pepper.

2 Divide the mixture between four scrubbed scallop shells or heatproof dishes. Sprinkle the breadcrumbs and remaining parsley on top and drizzle with the oil.

3 Place in the preheated oven and bake for 15–20 minutes, or until lightly golden and piping hot. Serve immediately.

FISH & OTHER SEAFOOD

CATALAN FISH STEW

Serves: 4   **Prep: 25 mins**   **Cook: 35–45 mins**

Ingredients

large pinch of saffron threads

4 tbsp boiling water

6 tbsp olive oil

1 large onion, chopped

2 garlic cloves, finely chopped

1½ tbsp chopped fresh thyme leaves

2 bay leaves

2 red peppers, cored, deseeded and coarsely chopped

800 g/1 lb 12 oz canned chopped tomatoes

1 tsp sweet smoked paprika

250 ml/9 fl oz fish stock

140 g/5 oz blanched almonds, toasted and finely ground

12–16 live mussels

12–16 live clams

600 g/1 lb 5 oz thick, boned hake or cod fillets, skinned and cut into 5-cm/2-inch chunks

12–16 uncooked prawns, heads and tails removed, deveined

salt and pepper

crusty bread, to serve

Method

1 Put the saffron in a heatproof bowl, add the water and set aside to infuse.

2 Heat the oil in a large, heavy-based flameproof casserole over a medium-high heat. Reduce the heat to low, add the onion and fry for 10 minutes, until golden, but not brown. Stir in the garlic, thyme, bay leaves and red peppers and continue frying for a further 5 minutes, or until the peppers are soft. Add the tomatoes and paprika and continue to simmer for 5 minutes, stirring frequently.

3 Stir in the stock, reserved saffron water and ground almonds and bring to the boil, stirring frequently. Reduce the heat and simmer for 5–10 minutes until the sauce reduces and thickens. Add salt and pepper to taste.

4 Meanwhile, prepare the mussels and clams. Cut off and discard any beards from the mussels, then scrub any dirty shells. Discard any with broken shells and those that do not close when tapped.

5 Gently stir in the hake so it doesn't break up and add the prawns, mussels and clams. Reduce the heat to very low, cover the casserole and simmer for about 5 minutes until the hake is cooked through, the prawns have turned pink and the mussels and clams have opened; discard any mussels or clams that remain closed. Serve at once with plenty of crusty bread for soaking up the juices.

STUFFED SQUID

Serves: 4

Prep: 35–40 mins,
plus soaking & cooling

Cook: 45 mins

Ingredients

8 sun-dried tomatoes

8 small prepared squid (bodies about 13 cm/ 5 inches long)

85 g/3 oz fresh white breadcrumbs

2 tbsp capers, rinsed and finely chopped

2 tbsp chopped fresh flat-leaf parsley

1 egg white

olive oil, for brushing and drizzling

3 tbsp dry white wine

salt and pepper

lemon wedges, to serve

Method

1 Put the tomatoes in a bowl, cover with boiling water and set aside to soak for 15–20 minutes. Meanwhile, finely chop the squid tentacles and place in another bowl. Add the breadcrumbs, capers and parsley.

2 Preheat the oven to 160°C/325°F/Gas Mark 3. Drain the tomatoes, pat dry with kitchen paper and finely chop. Add to the breadcrumb mixture mix and season to taste with salt and pepper. Stir in the egg white. Spoon the breadcrumb mixture into the squid body sacs, pushing down well. Do not fill them more than about three quarters full or they will burst during cooking. Secure the opening of each sac with a cocktail stick.

3 Generously brush oil over an ovenproof dish large enough to hold the squid snugly in a single layer. Place the squid in the dish and pour in the wine. Cover with foil and bake in the preheated oven for about 45 minutes, turning and basting occasionally. Test to check if the squid is tender.

4 Remove from the oven and set aside to cool to room temperature. To serve, remove and discard the cocktail sticks and slice the squid into rounds. Place on four warmed plates, drizzle with a little oil and the cooled cooking juices and serve with lemon wedges for squeezing over.

MEDITERRANEAN SWORDFISH

Serves: 4   **Prep: 15–20 mins**   **Cook: 45 mins**

Ingredients

2 tbsp olive oil

1 onion, finely chopped

1 celery stick, finely chopped

115 g/4 oz green olives, stoned

450 g/1 lb tomatoes, chopped

3 tbsp bottled capers, drained

4 swordfish steaks, about 140 g/5 oz each

salt and pepper

fresh flat-leaf parsley sprigs, to garnish

Method

1 Heat the oil in a large, heavy-based frying pan. Add the onion and celery and cook over a low heat, stirring occasionally, for 5 minutes, or until soft.

2 Meanwhile, roughly chop half the olives. Stir the chopped and whole olives into the saucepan with the tomatoes and capers and season to taste with salt and pepper.

3 Bring to the boil, then reduce the heat, cover and simmer gently, stirring occasionally, for 15 minutes.

4 Add the swordfish steaks to the pan and return to the boil. Cover and simmer for 20 minutes, or until the fish is cooked and the flesh flakes easily, turning once during cooking. Transfer the fish to serving plates and spoon the sauce over. Garnish with fresh parsley sprigs and serve immediately.

FISH & OTHER SEAFOOD

MUSSELS WITH PAPRIKA

Serves: 8   **Prep: 25 mins**   **Cook: 15–20 mins**

Ingredients

1 kg/2 lb 4 oz live mussels, scrubbed and debearded

4 tbsp Spanish olive oil

1 large fennel bulb, trimmed and very finely chopped

4 large garlic cloves, finely chopped

1 tbsp tomato purée

2 tsp Spanish hot or sweet paprika, to taste

250 ml/9 fl oz dry white wine

salt and pepper

sliced country-style bread, to serve

Method

1 Discard any mussels with broken shells and any that refuse to close when tapped.

2 Heat the oil in a large saucepan over a medium heat. Add the fennel and fry, stirring, for 3–5 minutes, until soft.

3 Stir in the garlic, tomato purée and paprika, reduce the heat and stir for a further minute. Pour in the wine and bring to the boil, stirring, until the liquid is reduced by half.

4 Reduce the heat, then add the mussels, cover the pan and steam for 3–5 minutes, until they open. Discard any mussels that remain closed. Season to taste with salt and pepper.

5 Remove the top shells, then transfer the mussels to a serving dish and pour over the cooking juices. Serve with plenty of bread.

★ Variation

Experiment with pepper-based spices such as cayenne or chilli powder, or for a completely different taste use mustard, garlic powder or ground ginger.

VEGETABLES, CHEESE & EGGS

ARTICHOKE & RED PEPPER TORTILLA

Serves: 6-8   **Prep: 25 mins**   **Cook: 22-28 mins**

Ingredients

250 g/9 oz drained artichoke hearts in oil, quartered and 2 tbsp oil reserved

175 g/6 oz drained grilled red peppers in oil, chopped and 2 tbsp oil reserved

1 large onion, thinly sliced

9 large eggs

Spanish olive oil, for frying

salt and pepper

Method

1 Heat the reserved oil from the artichokes and peppers in a 25-cm/10-inch frying pan over a high heat. Reduce the heat, add the onion and fry, stirring, for 8–10 minutes, until golden.

2 Beat the eggs in a large bowl. Stir in the artichoke hearts and red peppers and season to taste with salt and pepper.

3 Using a slotted spoon, transfer the onions to the bowl, leaving as much oil in the pan as possible.

4 Add enough olive oil to the pan to make it up to 4 tablespoons. Heat over a high heat, swirling so it coats the side of the pan.

5 Add the egg mixture and smooth the surface. Cook for 30 seconds, then reduce the heat to medium and cook for a further 5–7 minutes, shaking the pan occasionally, until the base is set.

6 Use a spatula to loosen the side of the tortilla.

7 Place a large plate over the top of the pan. Invert the pan and plate together so the tortilla drops on to the plate.

8 Add 1 tablespoon of olive oil to the pan and heat. Slide the tortilla into the pan, cooked side up. Continue cooking for 3–5 minutes, until the eggs are set and the base is golden brown.

9 Slide the tortilla on to a plate. Cut into wedges and serve hot, warm or at room temperature.

★ Variation

Omit the red peppers to pare down this recipe to its barest ingredients.

PATATAS BRAVAS

Serves: 6   **Prep: 20–25 mins**   **Cook: 35–45 mins**

Ingredients

2 tbsp Spanish olive oil, plus extra for shallow-frying

1 onion, finely chopped

2 garlic cloves, sliced

3½ tbsp dry white wine or dry sherry

400 g/14 oz canned chopped tomatoes

2 tsp white or red wine vinegar

1–2 tsp dried chilli flakes

2 tsp Spanish hot or sweet smoked paprika

1 kg/2 lb 4 oz potatoes, washed but not peeled and cut into chunks

Method

1 Heat the 2 tablespoons of oil in a large saucepan, add the onion and cook over a medium heat, stirring occasionally, for 5 minutes, or until softened. Add the garlic and cook, stirring, for 30 seconds.

2 Add the wine and bring to the boil. Add the tomatoes, vinegar, chilli flakes and paprika, reduce the heat and simmer, uncovered, for 10–15 minutes, until a thick sauce forms.

3 Using a hand-held blender, blend the sauce in the pan until smooth. Set aside.

4 In a large frying pan, heat enough oil to come about 2.5 cm/1 inch up the side of the pan. Add the potatoes and cook over a medium-high heat, turning occasionally, for 10–15 minutes, until golden brown.

5 Remove with a slotted spoon and drain on kitchen paper.

6 Meanwhile, gently reheat the sauce.

7 Transfer the potatoes to a warmed serving dish and drizzle over the sauce. Serve immediately.

CHARGRILLED VEGETABLE PLATTER

Serves: 8

Prep: 25 mins,
plus infusing

Cook: 25–30 mins

Ingredients

125 ml/4 fl oz Spanish olive oil

4 garlic cloves, roughly chopped

4 fresh thyme sprigs

1.5 kg/3 lb 5 oz fresh vegetables, such as asparagus, aubergines, courgettes, fennel, thick spring onions and red peppers

salt and pepper

Romesco sauce, to serve

Method

1 Put the oil, garlic and thyme into a bowl and set aside to infuse for at least 1 hour.

2 Hold each asparagus spear at each end and bend until the woody stalk snaps. Discard the broken ends. If the stalks are thick, cut them in half lengthways.

3 Trim the aubergines and courgettes and cut them lengthways into 5-mm/¼-inch slices.

4 Trim the fennel and slice crossways through the bulb. Trim the spring onions.

5 Quarter, core and deseed the red peppers.

6 Heat a ridged, cast-iron griddle pan over a high heat until very hot. Brush with a little of the garlic-infused oil.

7 Working in batches, add the vegetables to the pan, placing the red pepper pieces skin-side down. Sprinkle with salt and pepper and cook until they start to become tender.

8 Using tongs, turn the vegetables over and continue cooking until tender. Brush the pan with oil as needed.

9 Transfer the vegetables to a warmed platter as they are cooked and serve hot, warm or at room temperature with romesco sauce.

VEGETABLES, CHEESE & EGGS

ROASTED PEPPER SALAD

Serves: 8

Prep: 30–35 mins, plus cooling

Cook: 40 mins

Ingredients

3 red peppers

3 yellow peppers

5 tbsp Spanish extra virgin olive oil, plus extra for brushing

2 tbsp sherry vinegar

2 garlic cloves, chopped

pinch of sugar

1 tbsp capers, drained and rinsed

8 small black Spanish olives

2 tbsp chopped fresh marjoram, plus extra sprigs to garnish

salt and pepper

Method

1 Preheat the oven to 200°C/400°F/Gas Mark 6. Brush the peppers with oil and put in a roasting tin. Roast in the preheated oven for 30 minutes, then turn over and roast for a further 10 minutes, until the skins have blistered and blackened.

2 Using a slotted spoon, transfer the roasted peppers to a polythene bag and leave for 15 minutes, or until cool enough to handle.

3 Holding the peppers one at a time over a clean bowl, use a sharp knife to make a small hole in the base, then gently squeeze out the juices and set aside.

4 Peel, core and deseed the peppers, then cut them into neat, thin strips and arrange them attractively on a serving platter.

5 Add the oil, vinegar, garlic, sugar, and salt and pepper to taste to the reserved pepper juices. Whisk together until combined, then drizzle over the peppers.

6 Sprinkle over the capers, olives and chopped marjoram.

7 Garnish with marjoram sprigs and serve at room temperature.

VEGETABLES, CHEESE & EGGS

CATALAN SPINACH

Serves: 8

Prep: 20 mins,
plus soaking & cooling

Cook: 10–15 mins

Ingredients

4 tbsp raisins

900 g/2 lb spinach, rinsed

2 tbsp Spanish olive oil

1 large garlic clove, chopped

2 tbsp pine nuts

pinch of dried chilli flakes, or to taste

salt and pepper

Method

1 Soak the raisins in lukewarm water for 15 minutes. Drain well and set aside.

2 Meanwhile, put the spinach into a large saucepan with just the water clinging to the leaves. Turn the heat to high and stir for 3–5 minutes, until the spinach is very tender. Drain well. When cool enough to handle, squeeze out any excess water, then finely chop.

3 Heat the oil in a large frying pan over a medium heat. Add the garlic and fry, stirring, for 1–2 minutes, until golden. Stir in the raisins, pine nuts and chilli flakes and stir for 2 minutes, until the pine nuts are toasted.

4 Add the spinach and season to taste with salt and pepper. Increase the heat and stir for 3–5 minutes.

5 Spoon the spinach into a warm serving dish and serve immediately.

STEWED CHICKPEAS

Serves: 8   **Prep: 15 mins**   **Cook: 35–40 mins**

Ingredients

6 tbsp Spanish olive oil

1 large onion,
finely chopped

800 g/1 lb 12 oz canned
chopped tomatoes

4 large garlic cloves,
chopped

800 g/1 lb 12 oz canned
chickpeas, drained
and rinsed

1 tsp Spanish sweet paprika,
or to taste

salt and pepper

country-style bread,
to serve

Method

1 Heat the oil in a large saucepan over a medium heat. Add the onion, reduce the heat to low and fry, stirring, for 5–8 minutes, until soft.

2 Add the tomatoes and garlic and simmer for 10 minutes, stirring occasionally.

3 Stir in the chickpeas and paprika and season to taste with salt and pepper. Cover the pan and bring to the boil.

4 Reduce the heat to low and simmer, partially covered, for 15 minutes, until the chickpeas are coated in a thick sauce. Adjust the seasoning, adding salt and pepper if needed.

5 Spoon into a serving bowl and serve hot or at room temperature with bread.

VEGETABLES, CHEESE & EGGS

GAZPACHO

Serves: 4–6

Prep: 20–25 mins, plus chilling   **Cook: N/A**

Ingredients

500 g/1 lb 2 oz large, ripe tomatoes, peeled, deseeded and chopped

3 large red peppers, deseeded and chopped

2 tbsp sherry vinegar, or to taste

4 tbsp Spanish olive oil

salt and pepper

To serve

4–6 ice cubes

finely chopped mixed peppers, cucumber and hard-boiled eggs

Method

1 Put the tomatoes, red peppers, vinegar and oil into a food processor.

2 Process until blended and the mixture is as smooth or chunky as you like.

3 Cover and chill for at least 4 hours before serving.

4 Taste and adjust the seasoning, adding extra vinegar and salt and pepper if needed. Ladle the soup into bowls and add an ice cube to each.

5 To serve, put a selection of garnishes, such as finely chopped peppers, cucumber and hard-boiled eggs, in bowls and let everyone add their own.

VEGETABLES, CHEESE & EGGS

FLAMENCO EGGS

Serves: 4   **Prep: 20–25 mins**   **Cook: 35–45 mins**

Ingredients

4 tbsp Spanish olive oil

1 onion, thinly sliced

2 garlic cloves, finely chopped

2 small red peppers, deseeded and chopped

4 tomatoes, peeled, deseeded and chopped

1 tbsp chopped fresh parsley

200 g/7 oz canned sweetcorn kernels, drained

4 eggs

salt and cayenne pepper

Method

1 Preheat the oven to 180°C/350°F/Gas Mark 4. Heat the oil in a large, heavy-based frying pan. Add the onion and garlic and cook over a low heat, stirring occasionally, for 5 minutes, or until soft.

2 Add the red peppers and cook, stirring occasionally, for a further 10 minutes.

3 Stir in the tomatoes and parsley, season to taste with salt and cayenne pepper and cook for a further 5 minutes.

4 Stir in the sweetcorn and remove the pan from the heat.

5 Divide the mixture between four individual baking dishes. Use the back of a spoon to make a hollow in the centre of each portion.

6 Break an egg into each hollow. Bake in the preheated oven for 15–25 minutes, or until the eggs have set.

7 Serve the eggs hot and eat straight from the baking dishes.

VEGETABLES, CHEESE & EGGS

PISTO MANCHEGO

Serves: 8 **Prep: 25–30 mins** **Cook: 30–35 mins**

Ingredients

4 large tomatoes

1 red onion

1 aubergine, about 500 g/1 lb 2 oz

1 courgette

4 garlic cloves, peeled

2 green peppers

2 red peppers

125 ml/4 fl oz Spanish olive oil

2–3 tsp sherry vinegar, to taste

salt and pepper

crusty bread, to serve

Method

1 Cut an 'X' in the stem end of each tomato. Put the tomatoes into a large heatproof bowl and pour over enough boiling water to cover. Leave to stand for 30 seconds, or until the skins split.

2 Drain the tomatoes and immediately rinse under cold running water to cool. Use a small knife to peel off the skins.

3 Cut the tomatoes in half and use a teaspoon to scoop out the seeds and cores. Finely dice the flesh.

4 Peel the onion. Trim the aubergine and courgette. Finely chop the onion, aubergine, courgette and garlic.

5 Core, deseed and finely dice the peppers.

6 Heat the oil in a large frying pan over a medium heat. Add the onion and peppers and fry, stirring occasionally, for 8–10 minutes.

7 Stir in the garlic, tomatoes, aubergine and courgette. Bring to the boil, stirring, then reduce the heat and simmer for 15–20 minutes.

8 Season to taste with salt and pepper, stir in the vinegar, then transfer the vegetable mixture to a serving bowl and serve hot or at room temperature with bread.

BROAD BEAN & MUSHROOM SALAD

Serves: 8

Prep: 35–40 mins, plus standing & cooling

Cook: 10–12 mins

Ingredients

1 red onion

3 tbsp Spanish olive oil, plus extra to serve

900 g/2 lb chestnut mushrooms, sliced

500 g/1 lb 2 oz frozen broad beans

2 tbsp chopped fresh dill

sherry vinegar, to taste

salt and pepper

escarole leaves and sliced crusty bread, to serve

Method

1 Peel the onion, then cut into quarters and thinly slice. Sprinkle with salt and leave to soften.

2 Heat the oil in a frying pan over a high heat.

3 Add the mushrooms to the pan, season with salt and pepper and fry, stirring frequently, until they have absorbed the oil. Reduce the heat to low. When the juices have come out of the mushrooms, increase the heat and sauté for 4–5 minutes, stirring frequently, until the juices have almost evaporated. Then tip the mushrooms and any remaining liquid into a bowl.

4 Meanwhile, bring a saucepan of lightly salted water to the boil. Add the broad beans, bring back to the boil and cook for 4–5 minutes, until tender. Drain and immediately transfer to a bowl of iced water.

5 When the beans are cool enough to handle, drain and use your fingers to pop the beans out of their skins and add to the mushrooms. Leave to cool.

6 Rinse the onion, then pat dry with kitchen paper.

7 Add the onion and dill to the mushrooms and beans. Add a splash of vinegar and salt and pepper. Transfer to a platter lined with escarole leaves and serve with extra oil and bread.

VEGETABLES, CHEESE & EGGS

COURGETTE SALAD WITH CORIANDER DRESSING

Serves: 6

Prep: 25–30 mins, plus draining & cooling   **Cook: 25 mins**

Ingredients

500 g/1 lb 2 oz small courgettes

1 tsp salt

1 tbsp Spanish olive oil

1 garlic clove, crushed

50 g/1¾ oz pine nuts

Coriander dressing

2 garlic cloves, chopped

1 tsp ground cumin

8 tbsp chopped fresh coriander leaves

2 tbsp chopped fresh flat-leaf parsley

5 tbsp Spanish extra virgin olive oil

2 tbsp white wine vinegar

salt and pepper

Method

1 Thinly slice the courgettes lengthways. Layer the slices in a colander, sprinkling over a little salt, and set over a large plate. Leave to drain for about 1 hour.

2 Meanwhile, make the dressing. Put the garlic, cumin and herbs in a food processor and pulse until well mixed.

3 With the motor running, add 1 tablespoon of the extra virgin olive oil, drop by drop. Using a spatula, scrape down the side of the bowl. With the motor running again, very slowly add the remaining oil in a thin, steady stream until it has all been incorporated and the dressing has slightly thickened. Add the vinegar to the dressing and process for 1 minute until blended. Season to taste with salt and pepper.

4 When the courgettes have drained, quickly rinse the slices under cold running water, then dry well with kitchen paper or a clean tea towel. Put in a large bowl, add the olive oil and garlic and toss together lightly.

5 Heat a ridged griddle pan. Add the courgette slices, in batches in a single layer, and cook, turning once, for 5 minutes, or until tender. Transfer to a large serving bowl. Set aside and leave to cool slightly.

Sprinkle the pine nuts over the courgettes. If the dressing has separated, whisk it together, then drizzle some over the courgettes.

Serve the courgettes accompanied by the remaining dressing in a small serving bowl.

BABY LEEK & ASPARAGUS SALAD

Serves: 6

Prep: 25 mins, plus cooling & chilling

Cook: 30 mins

Ingredients

3 eggs

450 g/1 lb baby leeks, trimmed

225 g/8 oz fresh young asparagus spears, trimmed

150 ml/5 fl oz mayonnaise

2 tbsp sherry vinegar

1 garlic clove, crushed

salt and pepper

2 tbsp capers

Method

1 Put the eggs in a saucepan, cover with cold water and slowly bring to the boil. Reduce the heat and simmer gently for 10 minutes. Immediately drain the eggs and rinse under cold running water to cool. Gently tap the eggs to crack the shells and leave until cold.

2 Meanwhile, slice the leeks and asparagus into 9-cm/3½-inch lengths. Put both the vegetables in a saucepan of boiling water, return to the boil and boil for 12 minutes until just tender. Drain and rinse under cold running water, then drain well.

3 Put the mayonnaise in a large bowl, add the vinegar and garlic and mix together until smooth. Season to taste with salt and pepper. Add the leeks and asparagus to the dressing and toss together until well coated. Transfer the vegetables to a serving dish, cover and chill in the refrigerator for at least 1 hour.

4 Just before serving, crack the shells of the eggs all over and remove them. Slice the eggs into quarters and add to the salad. Sprinkle over the capers and serve.

VEGETABLES, CHEESE & EGGS

SIMMERED SUMMER VEGETABLES

Serves: 6–8   **Prep: 25 mins**   **Cook: 45–60 mins**

Ingredients

1 large aubergine

4 tbsp Spanish olive oil

1 onion, thinly sliced

2 garlic cloves, finely chopped

2 courgettes, thinly sliced

1 red pepper, cored, deseeded and thinly sliced

1 green pepper, cored, deseeded and thinly sliced

8 tomatoes, peeled, deseeded and chopped

salt and pepper

chopped fresh flat-leaf parsley, to garnish

slices thick country bread, to serve (optional)

Method

1 Cut the aubergine into 2.5-cm/1-inch cubes. Heat the oil in a large flameproof casserole, add the onion and cook over a medium heat, stirring occasionally, for 5 minutes, or until softened but not browned. Add the garlic and cook, stirring, for 30 seconds until softened.

2 Increase the heat to medium-high, add the aubergine cubes and cook, stirring occasionally, for 10 minutes, or until softened and beginning to brown. Add the courgettes and peppers and cook, stirring occasionally, for 10 minutes until softened. Add the tomatoes and season to taste with salt and pepper.

3 Bring the mixture to the boil, then reduce the heat, cover and simmer, stirring occasionally so that the vegetables do not stick to the base of the pan, for 15–20 minutes until tender. If necessary, uncover, increase the heat and cook to evaporate any excess liquid, as the mixture should be thick.

4 Serve hot or cold, garnished with chopped parsley and accompanied by bread slices for scooping up the vegetables, if desired.

VEGETABLES, CHEESE & EGGS

BAKED TOMATO NESTS

Serves: 4

Prep: 15–20 mins,
plus draining

Cook: 15–20 mins

Ingredients

4 large ripe tomatoes

salt and pepper

4 large eggs

4 tbsp double cream

4 tbsp grated aged Mahon, Manchego or Parmesan cheese

Method

1 Preheat the oven to 180°C/350°F/Gas Mark 4. Cut a slice off the tops of the tomatoes and, using a teaspoon, carefully scoop out the pulp and seeds without piercing the shells. Turn the tomato shells upside down on kitchen paper and leave to drain for 15 minutes. Season the insides of the shells with salt and pepper.

2 Place the tomatoes in an ovenproof dish just large enough to hold them in a single layer. Carefully break 1 egg into each tomato shell, then top with 1 tablespoon of cream and 1 tablespoon of grated cheese.

3 Bake in the preheated oven for 15–20 minutes, or until the eggs are just set. Serve hot.

VEGETABLES, CHEESE & EGGS

ORANGE & FENNEL SALAD

Serves: 4   **Prep: 25 mins**   **Cook: N/A**

Ingredients

4 large, juicy oranges

1 large fennel bulb,
very thinly sliced

1 mild white onion,
finely sliced

2 tbsp Spanish extra virgin
olive oil

12 plump black Spanish
olives, stoned and
thinly sliced

fresh red chilli, deseeded
and very thinly
sliced (optional)

finely chopped
fresh parsley

French bread, to serve

Method

1 Finely grate the rind from the oranges into a
bowl and reserve. Using a small, serrated knife,
remove all the white pith from the oranges,
working over a bowl to catch the juice. Cut the
oranges horizontally into thin slices.

2 Toss the orange slices with the fennel and onion
slices. Whisk the olive oil into the reserved orange
juice, then spoon over the oranges. Sprinkle the
olive slices over the top, add the chilli, if using,
then sprinkle with the orange rind and parsley.
Serve with slices of French bread.

SUMMER SALAD IN A TOMATO DRESSING

Serves: 4

Prep: 25–30 mins, plus cooling

Cook: 15 mins

Ingredients

4 eggs (optional)

100 g/3½ oz fine green beans

500 g/1 lb 2 oz cherry or baby plum tomatoes

1 green pepper, cored, deseeded and diced

1 yellow pepper, cored, deseeded and diced

4 small gherkins, sliced

50 g/1¾ oz stoned black Spanish olives, halved

1 tsp capers

Tomato dressing

6 firm tomatoes

1 garlic clove, chopped

6 tbsp Spanish extra virgin olive oil

3 tbsp sherry vinegar

½ tsp hot or sweet smoked Spanish paprika

pinch of sugar

salt

Method

1 Put the eggs, if using, in a saucepan, cover with cold water and slowly bring to the boil. Reduce the heat and simmer gently for 10 minutes. Immediately drain the eggs and rinse under cold running water to cool. Gently tap the eggs to crack the shells and leave until cold.

2 Meanwhile, cut the beans into 2.5-cm/1-inch lengths. Cook in a saucepan of boiling water for 2 minutes, then drain well, rinse under cold running water and leave until cold.

3 To make the dressing, coarsely grate the tomatoes into a food processor, discarding the skins left in your hands. Add the garlic, oil, vinegar, paprika and sugar and process until smooth. Season to taste with salt.

4 Put the cooled beans in a large serving bowl. Add the tomatoes and peppers and toss the vegetables together. Drizzle the dressing over the vegetables.

5 Scatter the gherkins, olives and capers into the salad. Just before serving, crack the shells of the eggs all over and remove them. Slice the eggs into quarters and add to the salad.

BABY POTATOES WITH AÏOLI

Serves: 4

Prep: 25–30 mins,
plus marinating &
optional chilling

Cook: 12–15 mins

Ingredients

450 g/1 lb baby
new potatoes

1 tbsp chopped fresh
flat-leaf parsley

salt

Aïoli

1 large egg yolk,
at room temperature

1 tbsp white wine vinegar or
lemon juice

2 large garlic cloves, peeled

salt and pepper

5 tbsp Spanish extra virgin
olive oil

5 tbsp sunflower oil

1 tbsp water

Method

1 To make the aïoli, place the egg yolk, vinegar or lemon juice, garlic and salt and pepper to taste in a food processor fitted with a metal blade and blend together. With the motor still running, very slowly add the olive oil, then the sunflower oil, drop by drop at first, then, when it begins to thicken, in a slow, steady stream until the mixture is thick and smooth. Alternatively, use a bowl and whisk to make the aïoli.

2 For this recipe, the aïoli should be quite thin to coat the potatoes.

3 To ensure this, blend in the water to form the consistency of sauce.

4 To prepare the potatoes, cut them in halves or quarters to make bite-sized pieces. If they are very small, you can leave them whole. Place the potatoes in a large saucepan of cold salted water and bring to the boil. Reduce the heat and simmer for 7 minutes, or until just tender. Drain well, then transfer to a large bowl.

5 While the potatoes are still warm, pour over the aïoli sauce and gently toss the potatoes in it. Adding the sauce to the potatoes while they are still warm will help them to absorb the garlic flavour. Leave for 20 minutes to allow the potatoes to marinate in the sauce.

VEGETABLES, CHEESE & EGGS

6 Transfer the potatoes with aïoli to a warmed serving dish, sprinkle over the parsley and salt to taste and serve warm. Alternatively, the dish can be prepared ahead and stored in the refrigerator, but return it to room temperature before serving.

PEPPERS WITH FIERY CHEESE

Serves: 6

Prep: 20 mins,
plus cooling & chilling

Cook: 8–10 mins

Ingredients

1 red pepper, halved and deseeded

1 orange pepper, halved and deseeded

1 yellow pepper, halved and deseeded

115 g/4 oz Afuega'l Pitu cheese or other hot spiced cheese, diced

1 tbsp clear honey

1 tbsp sherry vinegar

salt and pepper

Method

1 Preheat the grill to high. Place the peppers, skin-side up, in a single layer on a baking sheet. Cook under the hot grill for 8–10 minutes, or until the skins have blistered and blackened. Using tongs, transfer to a polythene bag, tie the top and leave to cool.

2 When the peppers are cool enough to handle, peel off the skin with your fingers or a knife and discard it. Place the peppers on a serving plate and sprinkle over the cheese.

3 Whisk the honey and vinegar together in a bowl and season to taste with salt and pepper. Pour the dressing over the peppers, cover and leave to chill until ready to serve.

GOAT'S CHEESE WITH HONEY & WALNUTS

Serves: 4   **Prep: 10–15 mins**   **Cook: N/A**

Ingredients

about 175 g/6 oz goat's cheese, such as Monte Enebro, in one piece

about 115 g/4 oz clear honey, such as orange-blossom or thyme-flavoured

100 g/3½ oz walnut halves, chopped

Method

1 Remove the cheese from the refrigerator at least 20 minutes before serving to allow it to come to room temperature.

2 Pour the honey into a bowl. Place the walnuts in another bowl.

3 Serve the cheese on a board with a cheese knife and let everyone cut a slice for themselves, drizzling over some honey, with a dipper, if available, and sprinkling with chopped walnuts.

4 Alternatively, cut the cheese into four quarters and place a slice on each of four serving plates. Drizzle over some honey, sprinkle with chopped nuts and serve.

SPANISH SPINACH & TOMATO PIZZAS

Makes: 32

Prep: 45 mins, plus standing & rising

Cook: 25–30 mins

Ingredients

2 tbsp Spanish olive oil, plus extra for brushing and drizzling

1 onion, finely chopped

1 garlic clove, finely chopped

400 g/14 oz canned chopped tomatoes

125 g/4½ oz baby spinach leaves

salt and pepper

25 g/1 oz pine nuts

Bread dough

100 ml/3½ fl oz warm water

½ tsp easy-blend dried yeast

pinch of sugar

200 g/7 oz strong white flour, plus extra for dusting

½ tsp salt

Method

1 To make the bread dough, measure the water into a small bowl, sprinkle in the dried yeast and sugar and leave in a warm place for 10–15 minutes, or until frothy.

2 Meanwhile, sift the flour and salt into a large bowl. Make a well in the centre of the flour and pour in the yeast liquid, then mix together with a wooden spoon. Using your hands, work the mixture until it leaves the sides of the bowl clean.

3 Turn the dough out on to a lightly floured work surface and knead for 10 minutes, or until smooth and elastic and no longer sticky. Shape into a ball and put it in a clean bowl. Cover with a clean, damp tea towel and leave in a warm place for 1 hour, or until it has risen and doubled in size.

4 To make the topping, heat the olive oil in a large, heavy-based frying pan. Add the onion and fry for 5 minutes, or until softened but not browned. Add the garlic and fry for a further 30 seconds. Stir in the tomatoes and cook for 5 minutes, letting them bubble and stirring occasionally, until reduced to a thick mixture. Add the spinach leaves and cook, stirring, until they have wilted a little. Season the mixture to taste with salt and pepper.

5 While the dough is rising, preheat the oven to 200°C/400°F/Gas Mark 6. Brush several baking trays with olive oil. Turn the dough out on to a lightly floured work surface and knead well for 2–3 minutes to knock out the air bubbles. Roll out the dough very, very thinly and, using a 6-cm/2½-inch plain, round cutter, cut out 32 rounds. Place on the prepared baking sheets.

6 Spread each base with the spinach mixture to cover, then sprinkle the pine nuts over the top. Drizzle a little olive oil over each pizza. Bake in the oven for 10–15 minutes, or until the edges of the dough are golden brown. Serve the spinach and tomato pizzas hot.

GREEN BEANS WITH PINE NUTS

Serves: 8 **Prep: 20 mins** **Cook: 20–25 mins**

Ingredients

2 tbsp Spanish olive oil

50 g/1¾ oz pine nuts

½ –1 tsp paprika

450 g/1 lb green beans

1 small onion, finely chopped

1 garlic clove, finely chopped

salt and pepper

juice of ½ lemon

Method

1 Heat the oil in a large, heavy-based frying pan, add the pine nuts and fry for about 1 minute, stirring all the time and shaking the pan, until light golden brown. Using a slotted spoon, remove the pine nuts from the pan, drain well on kitchen paper, then transfer to a bowl. Reserve the oil in the frying pan for later. Add the paprika, according to taste, to the pine nuts, stir together until coated, and then set aside.

2 Top and tail the green beans and remove any strings if necessary. Put the beans in a saucepan, pour over boiling water, return to the boil and cook for 5 minutes, or until tender but still firm. Drain well in a colander.

3 Reheat the oil in the frying pan, add the onion and fry for 5–10 minutes, or until softened and beginning to brown. Add the garlic and fry for a further 30 seconds.

4 Add the beans to the pan and cook for 2–3 minutes, tossing together with the onion until heated through. Season the beans to taste with salt and pepper.

5 Turn the contents of the pan into a warmed serving dish, sprinkle over the lemon juice and toss together. Scatter over the golden pine kernels and serve hot.

VEGETABLES, CHEESE & EGGS

STUFFED PIMIENTOS

Makes: 7–8   **Prep: 25 mins,**   **Cook: N/A**
plus chilling

Ingredients

185 g/6½ oz canned or
bottled whole chargrilled
sweet red peppers

salt and pepper

fresh herb sprigs, to garnish

Curd cheese
and herb

225 g/8 oz curd cheese

1 tsp lemon juice

1 garlic clove, crushed

4 tbsp chopped fresh
flat-leaved parsley

1 tbsp chopped fresh mint

1 tbsp chopped
fresh oregano

Tuna and mayonnaise

200 g/7 oz canned tuna
steak in olive oil, drained

5 tbsp mayonnaise

2 tsp lemon juice

2 tbsp chopped fresh
flat-leaved parsley

Goat's cheese
and olive

50 g/1¾ oz stoned black
olives, finely chopped

200 g/7 oz soft
goat's cheese

1 garlic clove, crushed

Method

1 Lift the peppers from the jar, reserving the oil for later. Select the filling you wish to make.

2 To make the curd cheese and herb filling, put the curd cheese in a bowl and add the lemon juice, garlic, parsley, mint and oregano. Mix well together. Season to taste with salt and pepper.

3 To make the tuna and mayonnaise filling, put the tuna in a bowl and add the mayonnaise, lemon juice and parsley. Add 1 tablespoon of the reserved oil from the jar of pimientos and mix well. Season to taste with salt and pepper.

4 To make the goat's cheese and olive filling, put the olives in a bowl and add the goat's cheese, garlic and 1 tablespoon of the reserved oil from the jar of pimientos. Mix well together. Season to taste with salt and pepper.

5 Using a teaspoon, heap the filling of your choice into each pimiento. Put in the refrigerator and chill for at least 2 hours until firm.

6 To serve the pimientos, arrange them on a serving plate and, if necessary, wipe with kitchen paper to remove any of the filling that has spread over the skins. Garnish with herb sprigs.

WHITE BEAN & PEPPER SALAD

Serves: 8

Prep: 25 mins,
plus optional chilling

Cook: N/A

Ingredients

2 large grilled red peppers in oil, drained and oil reserved

800 g/1 lb 12 oz canned haricot beans, butter beans or cannellini beans, drained and rinsed

2 spring onions, finely chopped

2 tbsp capers, drained and rinsed

2 tbsp sherry vinegar, or to taste

Spanish extra virgin olive oil, to taste

salt and pepper

crusty bread, to serve

Method

1 Cut the red peppers into long, thin strips, then transfer them to a bowl.

2 Add the beans, spring onions and capers and gently mix together.

3 Put 4 tablespoons of the reserved oil from the peppers and the vinegar into a bowl and season to taste with salt and pepper. Whisk until blended, then add extra vinegar or oil to taste.

4 Pour the dressing over the bean mixture and gently mix together.

5 Spoon the salad into a serving bowl and serve immediately or chill until required. Serve with plenty of bread.

POTATO WEDGES WITH SHALLOTS & ROSEMARY

Serves: 6   **Prep: 20–25 mins**   **Cook: 1 hour**

Ingredients

1 kg/2 lb 4 oz
large potatoes

salt and pepper

6 tbsp Spanish olive oil

2 fresh rosemary sprigs

150 g/5½ oz baby shallots

2 garlic cloves, sliced

Method

1 Preheat the oven to 200°C/400°F/Gas Mark 6.
Peel and cut each potato into 8 thick wedges.
Put the potatoes in a large saucepan of salted
water and bring to the boil. Reduce the heat
and simmer for 5 minutes.

2 Heat the oil in a large roasting tin on the hob.
Drain the potatoes well and add to the roasting
tin. Strip the leaves off the rosemary sprigs, finely
chop and sprinkle over the potatoes.

3 Roast the potatoes in the preheated oven for
35 minutes, turning twice during cooking. Add
the shallots and garlic and roast for a further
15 minutes until golden brown. Season to taste
with salt and pepper.

4 Transfer to a warmed serving dish and serve hot.

VEGETABLES, CHEESE & EGGS

SPINACH & MOZZARELLA OMELETTE

Serves: 4   **Prep: 15 mins**   **Cook: 6-8 mins**

Ingredients

1 tbsp butter

4 eggs, beaten lightly

40 g/1½ oz mozzarella cheese, thinly sliced and cut into bite-sized pieces

small handful baby spinach, stalks removed

salt and pepper

1 oil-cured red pepper, sliced into strips, to garnish

Method

1 Heat a 25-cm/10-inch non-stick pan over medium-high heat. Add the butter and when it sizzles, pour in the eggs. Season with salt and pepper, then stir gently with the back of a fork until large flakes form. Leave to cook for a few seconds then tilt the pan and lift the edges of the mixture with a spatula, so that uncooked egg flows underneath to cook evenly.

2 Scatter the cheese and spinach over the top, and leave to cook for a few seconds. Once the surface starts to solidify, carefully fold the omelette in half. Cook for a few seconds, pressing the surface with a spatula. Turn the omelette over and cook for another few seconds, until the cheese is soft and the spinach wilted.

3 Slip the omelette onto a warm serving dish and slice into segments. Garnish with strips of red pepper before serving.

TOMATO, MOZZARELLA & AVOCADO SALAD

Serves: 4 **Prep: 15–20 mins** **Cook: N/A**

Ingredients

2 ripe beef tomatoes

150 g/5½ oz fresh mozzarella

2 avocados

4 tbsp olive oil

1½ tbsp white wine vinegar

1 tsp coarse grain mustard

few fresh basil leaves, torn into pieces

20 black olives

salt and pepper

fresh crusty bread, to serve

Method

1 Using a sharp knife, cut the tomatoes into thick wedges and place in a large serving dish. Drain the mozzarella and roughly tear into pieces. Cut the avocados in half and remove the stones. Cut the flesh into slices, then arrange the mozzarella cheese and avocado with the tomatoes.

2 Mix the oil, vinegar and mustard together in a small bowl, add salt and pepper to taste, then drizzle over the salad.

3 Scatter the basil and olives over the top and serve immediately with fresh crusty bread.

MUSHROOMS WITH ROASTED GARLIC & SPRING ONIONS

Serves: 4   **Prep: 20 mins**   **Cook: 1 hour 25 mins**

Ingredients

2 garlic bulbs

2 tbsp olive oil

350 g/12 oz assorted mushrooms, such as chestnut, open-cap and chanterelles, halved if large

1 tbsp chopped fresh parsley

8 spring onions, cut into 2.5-cm/1-inch lengths

salt and pepper

Method

1 Preheat the oven to 180°C/350°F/Gas Mark 4. Slice off the tops of the garlic bulbs and press down to loosen the cloves. Place them in an ovenproof dish and season to taste with salt and pepper. Drizzle 2 teaspoons of the oil over the bulbs and roast for 30 minutes. Remove from the oven and drizzle with 1 teaspoon of the remaining oil. Return to the oven and roast for a further 45 minutes. Remove from the oven and leave until cool enough to handle, then peel the cloves.

2 Tip the oil from the dish into a heavy-based frying pan, add the remaining oil and heat. Add the mushrooms and cook over a medium heat, stirring frequently, for 4 minutes.

3 Add the garlic cloves, parsley and spring onions and cook, stirring frequently, for 5 minutes. Season to taste with salt and pepper and serve immediately.

FIGS WITH BLUE CHEESE

Serves: 6

Prep: 20–25 mins, plus cooling

Cook: 5–10 mins

Ingredients

butter, for greasing

Caramelized almonds

100 g/3½ oz caster sugar

115 g/4 oz blanched whole almonds

12 ripe figs

350 g/12 oz Spanish blue cheese, such as Picós, crumbled

Spanish extra virgin olive oil, for drizzling

Method

1 First make the caramelized almonds. Lightly grease a baking sheet. Place the sugar in a saucepan over a medium heat and stir until the sugar melts and turns golden brown and bubbles. Do not stir once the mixture begins to bubble. Remove the saucepan from the heat, add the almonds one at a time and quickly turn with a fork until coated. If the caramel hardens, return the saucepan to the heat. Transfer each almond to the greased baking sheet once it is coated. Leave until cool and firm.

2 To serve, slice the figs in half and arrange 4 halves on individual serving plates. Roughly chop the almonds by hand. Place a mound of blue cheese on each plate and sprinkle with chopped almonds. Drizzle the figs very lightly with the olive oil.

★ Variation

A soft goat's cheese would work really well as an alternative to the blue cheese.

TOPPINGS FOR BREADS & PASTRY FILLINGS

TOMATO BREAD

Serves: 2-4　　**Prep: 10-15 mins**　　**Cook: 4 mins,**
plus optional toasting

Ingredients

4 slices bread from
a long, thin loaf,
cut diagonally

2 ripe tomatoes, halved

1 garlic clove,
finely chopped

2 tbsp Spanish olive oil

Method

1 If the bread is soft, toast it under a preheated gril
until light golden on both sides.

2 Rub one side of each slice of bread with half
a tomato.

3 Sprinkle over the chopped garlic.

4 Drizzle the oil over the top.

5 Serve immediately, before the bread has time to
become soggy.

★ Variation

You can always leave out the garlic if you find
the taste overpowering. You can also experimen
with different types of bread such as pitta bread

TAPENADE

Serves: 4

Prep: 15–20 mins, plus chilling   **Cook: N/A**

Ingredients

100 g/3½ oz canned anchovy fillets in oil

350 g/12 oz black olives, stoned and roughly chopped

2 garlic cloves, roughly chopped

2 tbsp capers, drained and rinsed

1 tbsp Dijon mustard

3 tbsp Spanish extra virgin olive oil

2 tbsp lemon juice

slices of crusty bread, to serve

Method

1 Drain the anchovies, reserving the oil from the can.

2 Roughly chop the anchovies.

3 Place the anchovies in a food processor or blender.

4 Add the reserved oil and all the remaining ingredients.

5 Process to a smooth purée. Stop and scrape down the sides if necessary.

6 Transfer the tapenade to a dish, cover with clingfilm and chill in the refrigerator until required.

7 Bring to room temperature, remove the clingfilm and serve spread on slices of bread.

CHEESE & SUN-DRIED TOMATO TOASTS

Serves: 4–6

Prep: 15–20 mins,
plus standing

Cook: 10 mins

Ingredients

2 loaves of bread (such as pan rustico or pan de centeno)

175 ml/6 fl oz sun-dried tomato purée

300 g/10½ oz mozzarella, drained and diced

1½ tsp dried oregano

2–3 tbsp olive oil

pepper

Method

1 Slice the loaves diagonally and discard the end pieces. Toast the slices on both sides under a preheated grill until golden.

2 Spread one side of each toast with the sun-dried tomato purée and top with mozzarella. Sprinkle with oregano and season to taste with pepper.

3 Place the toasts on a large baking sheet and drizzle with olive oil. Bake in a preheated oven, 220°C/425°F/Gas Mark 7, for about 5 minutes, until the cheese has melted and is bubbling. Remove the hot toasts from the oven and leave them to stand for 5 minutes before serving.

RUSSIAN SALAD

Makes: 16–20

Prep: 30 mins,
plus cooling

Cook: 35–40 mins

Ingredients

2 eggs

350 g/12 oz new
potatoes, scrubbed

125 g/4½ oz carrots, peeled
and diced

125 g/4½ oz shelled fresh
peas or thawed frozen peas

4 spring onions,
finely chopped

125 ml/4 fl oz mayonnaise

1 tbsp chopped fresh dill

1 tsp Spanish sweet paprika,
or to taste

16–20 slices bread from
a long, thin loaf

salt and pepper

Method

1 Place the eggs in a saucepan and pour in
enough water to cover by 2.5 cm/1 inch. Bring to
the boil, then reduce the heat to low and simmer
for 9 minutes.

2 Drain the eggs and place under cold running
water until cool enough to handle. Shell the eggs
and finely chop the yolks and whites.

3 Bring a saucepan of lightly salted water to the
boil and add the potatoes. Bring back to the boil
and cook for 15–20 minutes, until tender.

4 Use a slotted spoon to remove the potatoes from
the water and place under cold running water
until cool enough to handle. Peel and cut into
5-mm/¼-inch dice, then set aside.

5 Add the carrots to the potato water, bring back
to the boil and cook for 2 minutes. Add the
peas and cook for a further 5 minutes if fresh,
or 3 minutes if thawed, until the vegetables are
tender. Drain well and leave to cool.

6 Beat the spring onions, mayonnaise, dill and
paprika in a large bowl. Add the vegetables and
eggs and gently mix together. Season to taste
with salt and pepper.

7 Mound the vegetable mixture on the bread
slices. Eat within 30 minutes.

SEAFOOD SALAD

Makes: 16–20   **Prep: 25 mins**   **Cook: N/A**

Ingredients

125 g/4½ oz drained canned small prawns

125 g/4½ oz drained canned white crabmeat

1 celery stick, very finely chopped

1 small red onion, very finely chopped

6 tbsp mayonnaise

lemon juice, to taste

2 tbsp finely chopped fresh parsley

16–20 slices bread from a long, thin loaf

Spanish sweet paprika, for dusting

salt and pepper

32–40 thin, short strips grilled red pepper in oil, drained, to garnish

Method

1 Put the prawns and crabmeat into a bowl and stir together.

2 Add the celery, onion, mayonnaise and lemon juice and stir together.

3 Season to taste with salt and pepper and stir in the parsley.

4 Mound the vegetable mixture on the bread slices and lightly dust with paprika.

5 Arrange on a serving platter and garnish each with two slices of red pepper arranged to form an 'X'. Serve within 30 minutes, before the bread has time to become soggy.

MIXED VEGETABLE BRUSCHETTA

Serves: 4　　　　　**Prep: 20 mins**　　　　**Cook: 30 mins**

Ingredients

olive oil, for brushing and drizzling

1 red pepper, halved and deseeded

1 orange pepper, halved and deseeded

4 thick slices baguette or ciabatta

1 fennel bulb, sliced

1 red onion, sliced

2 courgettes, sliced diagonally

2 garlic cloves, halved

1 tomato, halved

salt and pepper

fresh sage leaves, to garnish

Method

1 Brush a griddle pan with oil and preheat. Cut each pepper in half lengthways into 4 strips. Toast the bread slices on both sides in a toaster or under a grill.

2 When the griddle is hot add the peppers and fennel and cook for 4 minutes, then add the onion and courgettes and cook for a further 5 minutes, until all the vegetables are tender but still with a slight 'bite'. If necessary, cook the vegetables in 2 batches, as they should be placed on the griddle in a single layer.

3 Meanwhile, rub the garlic halves over the toasts, then rub them with the tomato halves. Place on warm plates. Pile the grilled vegetables on top of the toasts, drizzle with olive oil and season with salt and pepper. Garnish with sage and serve immediately on a warmed plate.

★ Variation

Experiment with a variety of different salad vegetables and different coloured peppers.

CHORIZO & QUAIL EGG TOASTS

Serves: 6　　　　**Prep: 20 mins**　　　　**Cook: 10 mins**

Ingredients

12 slices French bread, sliced on the diagonal, about 5 mm/¼ inch thick

about 40 g/1½ oz cured, ready-to-eat chorizo, cut into thin slices

olive oil

12 quail eggs

mild paprika

salt and pepper

Method

1 Preheat the grill to high. Arrange the slices of bread on a baking sheet and grill until golden brown on both sides.

2 Cut or fold the chorizo slices to fit on the toasts; set aside. Heat a thin layer of oil in a large frying pan over a medium heat until a cube of day-old bread sizzles – this takes about 40 seconds. Break the eggs into the frying pan and fry, spooning the fat over the yolks, until the whites are set and the yolks are cooked to your liking.

3 Remove the fried eggs from the frying pan and drain on kitchen paper. Immediately transfer to the chorizo-topped toasts and dust with paprika. Sprinkle with salt and pepper to taste, and serve at once.

SALT COD ON GARLIC TOASTS

Serves: 6

Prep: 30 mins,
plus soaking & cooling

Cook: 30 mins

Ingredients

200 g/7 oz dried salt cod
5 garlic cloves
225 ml/8 fl oz olive oil
225 ml/8 fl oz double cream
pepper
6 thick slices country bread

Method

1 Soak the dried salt cod in cold water for 48 hours, changing the water 3 times a day. Drain well, then cut into chunks and place in a large frying pan. Pour in enough cold water to cover and bring to a simmer. Poach for 8–10 minutes, or until tender. Drain and leave until cool enough to handle.

2 Finely chop 4 of the garlic cloves. Halve the remaining clove and reserve until required.

3 Remove and discard the skin from the fish. Roughly chop the flesh and place in a food processor or blender.

4 Pour the olive oil into a saucepan and add the chopped garlic. Bring to a simmer over a low heat. Pour the cream into a separate saucepan and bring to simmering point over a low heat. Remove both saucepans from the heat.

5 Process the fish briefly. With the motor still running, add a little of the garlic oil and process. With the motor still running, add a little cream and process. Continue in this way until all the garlic oil and cream have been used. Scrape the mixture into a serving bowl and season with pepper.

6 Toast the bread on both sides, then rub each slice with the cut sides of the reserved garlic. Pile the fish mixture onto the toasts and serve.

PRAWN & HARICOT TOASTIES

Serves: 4   **Prep: 20 mins**   **Cook: 15 mins**

Ingredients

3 garlic cloves

4 tbsp Spanish olive oil

1 Spanish onion, halved and finely chopped

400 g/14 oz canned haricot beans, drained and rinsed

4 tomatoes, diced

salt and pepper

4 thick slices country bread

280 g/10 oz cooked peeled prawns

watercress, to garnish

Method

1 Halve 1 of the garlic cloves and reserve. Finely chop the remaining cloves. Heat 2 tablespoons of the olive oil in a large, heavy-based frying pan. Add the chopped garlic and onion and cook over a low heat, stirring occasionally, for 5 minutes, or until softened.

2 Stir in the beans and tomatoes and season to taste with salt and pepper. Cook gently for a further 5 minutes.

3 Meanwhile, toast the bread on both sides, then rub each slice with the cut sides of the reserved garlic and drizzle with the remaining oil.

4 Stir the prawns into the bean mixture and heat through gently for 2–3 minutes. Pile the bean and prawn mixture onto the toasts and serve immediately, garnished with watercress.

ROMAN DIP WITH ANCHOVY ROUNDS

Serves: 4

Prep: 25 mins, plus cooling & chilling

Cook: 20 mins

Ingredients

1 egg

150 g/5½ oz stoned black Spanish olives

50 g/1¾ oz canned anchovy fillets in olive oil, drained and oil reserved

2 garlic cloves, 1 crushed and 1 peeled but kept whole

1 tbsp capers

½ tsp hot or sweet smoked Spanish paprika

1 tbsp Spanish brandy or sherry

4 tbsp Spanish extra virgin olive oil

pepper

1 small French loaf

Method

1 Put the egg in a saucepan, cover with cold water and slowly bring to the boil. Reduce the heat and simmer gently for 10 minutes. Drain the egg and rinse under cold running water to cool. Tap the egg to crack the shell and leave until cold.

2 When the egg is cold, crack the shell all over and remove it. Put the egg in a food processor and add the olives, 2 of the anchovy fillets, the crushed garlic, capers, paprika and brandy and process to a rough paste. With the motor running slowly add 1 tablespoon of the reserved oil from the anchovies and the extra virgin olive oil in a thin, steady stream. Season the dip with pepper.

3 Turn the dip into a small serving bowl, cover and chill in the refrigerator until ready to serve. To make the anchovy rounds, put the remaining anchovy fillets, remaining reserved oil from the anchovies and garlic clove in a mortar and, using a pestle, pound together to a paste. Turn the paste into a bowl, cover and chill in the refrigerator until ready to serve.

4 When ready to serve, preheat the grill to high. Slice the French bread into 2.5-cm/1-inch rounds and toast under the grill until golden brown on both sides. Spread the anchovy paste very thinly on the toasted bread and serve with the dip.

ASPARAGUS SCRAMBLED EGGS

Serves: 6   **Prep: 15–20 mins**   **Cook: 14–18 mins**

Ingredients

450 g/1 lb asparagus, trimmed and roughly chopped

2 tbsp Spanish olive oil

1 onion, finely chopped

1 garlic clove, finely chopped

6 eggs

1 tbsp water

salt and pepper

6 small slices country bread

Method

1 Steam the asparagus pieces for 8 minutes or cook in a large saucepan of boiling salted water for 4 minutes, or until just tender, depending on their thickness. Drain well, if necessary.

2 Meanwhile, heat the oil in a large frying pan, add the onion and cook over a medium heat, stirring occasionally, for 5 minutes, or until softened but not browned. Add the garlic and cook, stirring, for 30 seconds until softened.

3 Stir the asparagus into the frying pan and cook, stirring occasionally, for 3–4 minutes. Meanwhile, break the eggs into a bowl, add the water and beat together. Season to taste with salt and pepper.

4 Preheat the grill to high. Add the beaten eggs to the asparagus mixture and cook, stirring constantly, for 2 minutes, or until the eggs have just set. Remove from the heat.

5 Toast the bread slices under the grill until golden brown on both sides. Pile the scrambled eggs on top of the toast and serve immediately.

TOPPINGS FOR BREADS & PASTRY FILLINGS

LITTLE BREADS WITH BEAN PURÉE

Serves: 4

Prep: 15–20 mins, plus soaking & cooling

Cook: 1 hour 40 mins

Ingredients

225 g/8 oz dried haricot beans

½ onion, finely chopped

2 tbsp olive oil

2 tbsp chopped fresh mint

4 thick slices country bread

salt and pepper

Method

1 Place the beans in a bowl and add enough cold water to cover. Leave to soak for 4 hours, or preferably overnight, then drain.

2 Place the beans in a saucepan and add the onion. Pour in enough water to cover and bring to the boil. Cook for 1½ hours, or until tender, then drain well and leave to cool slightly.

3 Toast the bread on both sides. Transfer the beans to a food processor or blender and process to a purée. Scrape into a serving bowl and stir in the olive oil and mint. Season to taste with salt and pepper. Divide the purée between the slices of toast and serve at room temperature.

TOPPINGS FOR BREADS & PASTRY FILLINGS

CATALAN TOAST

Serves: 8   **Prep: 20 mins**   **Cook: 5 mins**

Ingredients

2 garlic cloves

2 large tomatoes

8 slices day-old French bread, about 2 cm/¾ inch thick

8 slices Serrano ham

8 slices Manchego cheese

3 tbsp Spanish extra virgin olive oil

pepper

Method

1 Preheat the grill to high. Halve the garlic cloves. Coarsely grate the tomatoes into a bowl, discarding the skins left in your hand, and season to taste with pepper.

2 Toast the bread slices under the grill until lightly golden brown on both sides. While the bread slices are still warm, rub with the cut side of the garlic halves to flavour, then top with the grated tomatoes. Add a slice of ham and a slice of cheese to each bread slice. Drizzle each with a little of the oil and serve immediately.

★ Variation

For even more flavour and colour, add roasted red peppers to each slice before adding the olive oil.

TOPPINGS FOR BREADS & PASTRY FILLINGS

FRESH MINT & BEAN PÂTÉ

Serves: 12

Prep: 40 mins,
plus cooling & chilling

Cook: 15 mins

Ingredients

800 g/1 lb 12 oz fresh broad beans in their pods, shelled to give about 350 g/12 oz

225 g/8 oz soft goat's cheese

1 garlic clove, crushed

2 spring onions, finely chopped

1 tbsp Spanish extra virgin olive oil, plus extra to serve

grated rind and 2 tbsp lemon juice

about 60 large fresh mint leaves, about 15 g/½ oz in total

salt and pepper

12 slices French bread

Method

1 Cook the broad beans in a saucepan of boiling water for 8–10 minutes until tender. Drain well and leave to cool. When the beans are cool enough to handle, slip off their skins and put the beans in a food processor. This is a laborious task, but worth doing if you have the time. This quantity will take about 15 minutes to skin.

2 Add the goat's cheese, garlic, spring onions, oil, lemon rind and juice and mint leaves to the broad beans and process until well mixed. Season the pâté to taste with salt and pepper. Turn into a bowl, cover and chill in the refrigerator for at least 1 hour before serving.

3 To serve, preheat the grill to high. Toast the bread slices under the grill until golden brown on both sides. Drizzle a little oil over the toasted bread slices, spread the pâté on top and serve immediately.

TOPPINGS FOR BREADS & PASTRY FILLINGS

WILD MUSHROOM & AÏOLI TOASTS

Serves: 6   **Prep: 15–20 mins**   **Cook: 15 mins**

Ingredients

5 tbsp Spanish olive oil

2 large garlic cloves, finely chopped

450 g/1 lb wild mushrooms, sliced

2 tbsp dry Spanish sherry

4 tbsp chopped fresh flat-leaf parsley

salt and pepper

12 slices long, thick crusty bread

8 tbsp Aïoli

Method

1 Heat the oil in a large frying pan, add the garlic and cook over a medium heat, stirring, for 30 seconds until softened. Increase the heat to high, add the mushrooms and cook, stirring constantly, until the mushrooms are coated in the oil and all the oil has been absorbed.

2 Reduce the heat to low and cook for 2–3 minutes until all the juices have been released from the mushrooms. Add the sherry, increase the heat to high again and cook, stirring frequently, for 3–4 minutes until the liquid has evaporated. Stir in the parsley and season to taste with salt and pepper.

3 Meanwhile, preheat the grill to high. Toast the bread slices under the grill until lightly golden brown on both sides.

4 Spread the aïoli on top of each toast and top with the cooked mushrooms. Carefully transfer the toasts to a grill rack and cook under the grill until the aïoli starts to bubble. Serve hot.

★ Variation

You can replace the wild mushrooms with others such as button, chestnut and/or flat mushrooms.

FLATBREAD WITH VEGETABLES & CLAMS

Serves: 4–6

Prep: 40 mins, plus rising, cooling & standing

Cook: 50 mins

Ingredients

2 tbsp Spanish extra virgin olive oil

4 large garlic cloves, crushed

2 large onions, thinly sliced

10 pimientos del piquillo, drained, patted dry and thinly sliced

250 g/9 oz shelled baby clams in brine (weight in jar), drained and rinsed

salt and pepper

Bread Dough

400 g/14 oz strong white flour, plus extra for dusting

1 sachet easy-blend dried yeast

1 tsp salt

½ tsp sugar

1 tbsp Spanish olive oil, plus extra for oiling

1 tbsp dry white wine

225 ml/8 fl oz warm water

Method

1 To make the dough, stir the flour, yeast, salt and sugar together in a bowl, making a well in the centre. Add the olive oil and wine to the water, then pour 175 ml/6 fl oz of the liquid into the well. Gradually mix in the flour from the sides, adding the remaining liquid if necessary, until a soft dough forms.

2 Turn out the dough onto a lightly floured surface and knead until smooth. Shape the dough into a ball. Wash the bowl and rub the inside with olive oil. Return the dough to the bowl and roll it around so that it is lightly coated in oil. Cover the bowl tightly with clingfilm and leave in a warm place until the dough doubles in size.

3 Heat the olive oil in a large, heavy-based frying pan over a medium heat. Reduce the heat, add the garlic and onions and fry slowly, stirring frequently, for 25 minutes, or until the onions are golden brown but not burned.

4 Preheat the oven to 230°C/450°F/Gas Mark 8. Transfer the onions to a bowl and leave to cool. Add the pimiento del piquillo strips and clams to the bowl and stir together. Reserve.

5 Punch the dough and knead quickly on a lightly floured work surface. Cover it with the upturned bowl and leave for 10 minutes, which will make it easier to roll out.

6 Heavily flour a 32 x 32-cm/12¾ x 12¾-inch shallow baking tray. Roll out the dough to make a 34-cm/13½-inch square and transfer it to the baking tray, rolling the edges to form a thin rim. Prick the base all over with a fork.

7 Spread the topping evenly over the dough and season to taste with salt and pepper. Bake in the preheated oven for 25 minutes, or until the rim is golden brown and the onion tips are slightly tinged. Transfer to a wire rack to cool completely. Cut into 12–16 slices.

ARTICHOKE & PIMIENTO FLATBREAD

Serves: 4

Prep: 40 mins, plus rising & cooling

Cook: 32–37 mins

Ingredients

4 tbsp Spanish olive oil, plus extra for oiling

2 large onions, thinly sliced

2 garlic cloves, finely chopped

400 g/14 oz canned artichoke hearts, drained and quartered

320 g/11¼ oz bottled or canned pimientos del piquillo, drained and thinly sliced

salt and pepper

40 g/1½ oz stoned black Spanish olives (optional)

Bread dough

400 g/14 oz strong white flour, plus extra for dusting

1½ tsp easy-blend dried yeast

1 tsp salt

½ tsp caster sugar

175 ml/6 fl oz warm water

3 tbsp Spanish olive oil

Method

1 To make the bread dough, put the flour, yeast, salt and sugar in a large bowl and make a well in the centre. Mix the water and oil together in a jug, pour into the well and gradually mix in the flour from the side. Using your hands, mix together to form a soft dough that leaves the side of the bowl clean.

2 Turn out the dough onto a lightly floured work surface and knead for 10 minutes, or until smooth and elastic and no longer sticky. Shape the dough into a ball and put in a clean bowl. Cover with a clean, damp tea towel and leave in a warm place for 1 hour, or until the dough has risen and doubled in size.

3 Meanwhile, heat 3 tablespoons of the oil in a large frying pan, add the onions and cook over a medium heat, stirring occasionally, for 10 minutes, or until golden brown. Add the garlic and cook, stirring, for 30 seconds until softened. Leave to cool. When cool, stir in the artichoke hearts and pimientos del piquillo, then season to taste with salt and pepper.

4 Preheat the oven to 200°C/400°F/Gas Mark 6. Oil a large baking sheet. Turn out the risen dough onto a lightly floured surface and knead lightly for 2–3 minutes to knock out the air. Roll out the dough to a 30-cm/12-inch square and transfer to the prepared baking sheet.

5 Brush the remaining oil over the dough and spread the artichoke and pimiento mixture on top. Sprinkle over the olives, if using. Bake in the preheated oven for 20–25 minutes until golden brown and crisp. Cut into 12 slices and serve hot or warm.

SUN-DRIED TOMATO TOASTS WITH GOAT'S CHEESE

Serves: 4

Prep: 20–25 mins, plus cooling & chilling

Cook: 10 mins

Ingredients

2 tbsp Spanish extra virgin olive oil, plus extra for oiling

225 g/8 oz soft goat's cheese

2 tsp freshly squeezed lemon juice

2 garlic cloves, crushed

1 tsp hot or sweet smoked Spanish paprika

25 g/1 oz stoned green Spanish olives, finely chopped

1 tbsp chopped fresh flat-leaf parsley

Sun-dried tomato toasts

50 g/1¾ oz sun-dried tomatoes in oil, drained and 3 tbsp oil reserved

1 garlic clove, crushed

1 long French loaf

Method

1 Preheat the oven to 200°C/400°F/Gas Mark 6. Generously oil a baking sheet. To make the toasts, very finely chop the tomatoes and put in a bowl. Add the reserved oil from the tomatoes and the garlic and mix together well.

2 Slice the bread into 1-cm/½-inch thick slices and spread with the tomato mixture. Put on the prepared baking sheet and bake in the preheated oven for 10 minutes, or until golden brown and crisp. Leave to cool on a wire rack.

3 To make the dip, put the goat's cheese in a food processor. With the motor running, add 1 tablespoon of the oil, drop by drop. Using a spatula, scrape down the side of the bowl. With the motor running again, very slowly add the remaining oil and the lemon juice in a thin, steady stream. Add the garlic and paprika and process until well mixed.

4 Stir the olives and parsley into the dip. Turn the dip into a small serving bowl, cover and chill in the refrigerator for at least 1 hour before serving.

5 Serve the dip accompanied by the toasts.

FRIED CHEESE PASTRIES

Makes: 25

Prep: 40 mins,
plus cooling & chilling

Cook: 25–30 mins

Ingredients

200 g/7 oz plain flour,
plus extra for dusting

2 eggs, lightly beaten

2 tbsp olive oil

1–2 tbsp cold water

1 egg white, beaten until
slightly frothy

vegetable oil for
deep-frying

salt

Filling

125 g/4½ oz ricotta cheese

1 egg, lightly beaten

70 g/2½ oz mozzarella
cheese, diced finely

25 g/1 oz Parmesan cheese,
diced finely

40 g/1½ oz salami or Parma
ham, chopped finely

1 tbsp chopped fresh
flat-leaf parsley

salt and pepper

Method

1 To make the filling, mix all the ingredients together in a bowl and season to taste. Sift the flour into a large bowl. Make a well in the centre and pour in the eggs. Add the oil and a pinch of salt. Stir with a fork, gradually drawing in the flour from around the edge. Once a dough has formed, knead for about 10 minutes, until smooth and silky. Wrap the dough in cling film and leave to rest in the refrigerator for at least 30 minutes or overnight.

2 Roll out the dough very thinly and, using a pastry cutter, stamp out circles about 7 cm/2¾ inches in diameter, re-rolling the dough until it is all used. Place the circles on a clean tea towel. Wet the edges of the circles with egg white. Place a teaspoon of filling in the middle, then fold over one half to form a semicircle.

3 Press the edges together, making sure they stick. Leave the filled pastries on the tea towel to rest for 30 minutes.

4 Heat the vegetable oil in a deep-fat fryer or large saucepan and drop the pastries into the hot oil, a few at a time, deep-frying for about 3–5 minutes. Remove from the pan and drain on crumpled kitchen paper. Serve at once while still hot.

AUBERGINE & PEPPER DIP

Serves: 6–8

Prep: 30 mins,
plus cooling & optional
chilling

Cook: 52 mins

Ingredients

2 large aubergines

2 red peppers

4 tbsp Spanish olive oil

2 garlic cloves,
roughly chopped

grated rind and juice of
½ lemon

1 tbsp chopped fresh
coriander, plus extra sprigs
to garnish

½ –1 tsp paprika

salt and pepper

bread or toast, to serve

Method

1 Preheat the oven to 190°C/ 375°F/Gas Mark 5.
Prick the skins of the aubergines and peppers all
over with a fork and brush with 1 tablespoon of
the olive oil. Place on a baking tray and bake in
the preheated oven for 45 minutes, or until the
skins are beginning to turn black, the flesh of the
aubergine is very soft and the peppers
are deflated.

2 When the vegetables are cooked, place them
in a bowl and cover tightly with a clean, damp
tea towel. Alternatively, place the vegetables in
a polythene bag and leave for about 15 minutes
until cool enough to handle.

3 When the vegetables have cooled, cut the
aubergines in half lengthways, carefully scoop
out the flesh and discard the skin. Cut the
aubergine flesh into large chunks. Remove
and discard the stem, core and seeds from the
peppers and cut the flesh into large pieces.

4 Heat the remaining olive oil in a frying pan. Add
the aubergine and pepper and fry for 5 minutes.
Add the garlic and fry for 30 seconds.

5 Turn the contents of the frying pan onto kitchen paper to drain, then transfer to a food processor. Add the lemon rind and juice, the chopped coriander, the paprika, and salt and pepper to taste, then process until a speckled purée is formed.

6 Transfer the aubergine and pepper dip to a serving bowl. Serve warm, at room temperature, or leave to cool for 30 minutes, then leave to chill in the refrigerator for at least 1 hour and serve cold. Garnish with coriander sprigs and accompany with thick slices of bread or toast for dipping.

PEPPERED PORK BRUSCHETTA

Serves: 4-6

Prep: 25–30 mins, plus marinating

Cook: 10 mins

Ingredients

350 g/12 oz pork fillet, cut crossways into 12 slices

1 small sourdough loaf

5 tbsp olive oil, plus extra for brushing the bread

2 tomatoes, sliced

2 large gherkins, diagonally sliced

Marinade

1 tsp black peppercorns

1 tsp fennel seeds

1 tsp paprika

½ tsp sea salt flakes

2 garlic cloves, chopped

grated zest of ½ lemon

1 tbsp olive oil

Method

1 Place the pork slices between two sheets of clingfilm and flatten with a mallet until thin.

2 Grind the marinade ingredients to a paste, using a mortar and pestle. Rub the paste into the meat and leave to marinate for 30 minutes at room temperature or overnight in the refrigerator. Allow to come to room temperature before cooking.

3 Slice the bread into six 1-cm/½-inch slices, using the wider part of the loaf. Lightly toast on both sides. Brush one side with oil and cut each slice in half. Set aside and keep warm.

4 Heat a large frying pan over a medium–high heat. Pour in the oil, add the pork and fry, in batches if necessary, for 1 minute on each side.

5 Place a tomato slice on each piece of toast, and top with the pork. Finish with a gherkin slice and serve warm or at room temperature.

ROASTED RED PEPPERS ON GARLIC TOASTS

Serves: 4

Prep: 25 mins, plus cooling

Cook: 50–55 mins

Ingredients

4 thin slices white country bread

5 tbsp Spanish olive oil

2 large garlic cloves, crushed

3 large red peppers

pepper

chopped fresh flat-leaf parsley, to garnish

Method

1 Preheat the oven to 230°C/450°F/Gas Mark 8. To make the garlic toasts, halve each bread slice. Put 3 tablespoons of the oil in a bowl and stir in the garlic. Brush each side of the bread slice halves with the oil mixture and transfer to a baking sheet. Bake in the preheated oven for 10–15 minutes until crisp and golden brown. Leave to cool on kitchen paper.

2 Reduce the oven temperature to 200°C/400°F/Gas Mark 6. Brush the red peppers with the remaining oil and put in a roasting tin. Roast in the oven for 30 minutes, turn over and roast for a further 10 minutes until the skins have blistered and blackened.

3 Using a slotted spoon, transfer the roasted peppers to a polythene bag and leave for 15 minutes, or until cool enough to handle.

4 Using a sharp knife or your fingers, carefully peel away the skin from the peppers. Halve the peppers and remove the stems, cores and seeds, then cut each pepper into neat, thin strips.

5 To serve, arrange the pepper strips on top of the garlic toasts. Season to taste with pepper and sprinkle with chopped parsley to garnish.

TOPPINGS FOR BREADS & PASTRY FILLINGS

POTATO & SPINACH TRIANGLES

Serves: 4　　　　**Prep: 30 mins**　　　　**Cook: 30 mins**

Ingredients

2 tbsp butter, melted, plus extra for greasing

225 g/8 oz waxy potatoes, finely diced

500 g/1 lb 2 oz fresh baby spinach

2 tbsp water

1 tomato, deseeded and chopped

¼ tsp chilli powder

½ tsp lemon juice

225 g/8 oz (8 sheets) filo pastry, thawed if frozen

salt and pepper

Method

1 Preheat the oven to 190°C/375°F/Gas Mark 5. Lightly grease a baking tray with a little butter. Cook the potatoes in a saucepan of lightly salted boiling water for 10 minutes, or until tender. Drain thoroughly and place in a mixing bowl.

2 Meanwhile, put the spinach into a large saucepan with the water, cover and cook, stirring occasionally, over a low heat for 2 minutes, or until wilted. Drain the spinach thoroughly, squeezing out the excess moisture, and add to the potatoes. Stir in the tomato, chilli powder and lemon juice. Season to taste with salt and pepper.

3 Lightly brush the sheets of filo pastry with melted butter. Spread out 4 of the sheets and lay a second sheet on top of each. Cut them into rectangles measuring about 20 x 10 cm/ 8 x 4 inches.

4 Spoon a portion of the potato and spinach mixture onto one end of each rectangle. Fold a corner of the pastry over the filling, fold the pointed end back over the pastry strip, then fold over the remaining pastry to form a triangle.

5 Place the triangles on the prepared baking sheet and bake in the preheated oven for 20 minutes, or until golden brown. Serve hot or cold.

TOPPINGS FOR BREADS & PASTRY FILLINGS

CROSTINI ALLA FIORENTINA

Serves: 6

Prep: 25 mins,
plus cooling

Cook: 30–35 mins

Ingredients

3 tbsp olive oil

1 onion, chopped

1 celery stick, chopped

1 carrot, chopped

1–2 garlic cloves, crushed

125 g/4½ oz chicken livers

125 g/4½ oz calf's liver

150 ml/¼ pint red wine

1 tbsp tomato purée

2 tbsp chopped
fresh parsley

3–4 canned anchovy fillets,
chopped finely

2 tbsp stock or water

25–40 g/1–1½ oz butter

1 tbsp capers

salt and pepper

small pieces of fried crusty
bread, to serve

chopped parsley, to garnish

Method

1 Heat the oil in a pan, add the onion, celery,
carrot and garlic, and cook gently for 4–5
minutes, or until the onion is soft but not coloured.

2 Meanwhile, trim the chicken livers and slice the
calf's liver into strips. Dry the calf's liver, and slice
into strips. Add the liver to the pan and fry gently
for a few minutes, until the strips are well sealed
on all sides.

3 Add half of the wine and cook until it has mostly
evaporated. Then add the rest of the wine, the
tomato purée, half of the parsley, the anchovy
fillets, stock or water, a little salt and plenty of
black pepper.

4 Cover the pan and leave to simmer, stirring
occasionally, for 15–20 minutes, or until tender
and most of the liquid has been absorbed.

5 Leave the mixture to cool a little, then either
coarsely mince or put into a food processor
and process to a chunky purée.

TOPPINGS FOR BREADS & PASTRY FILLINGS

6 Return to the pan and add the butter, capers and remaining parsley. Heat through gently until the butter melts. Adjust the seasoning and turn out into a bowl. Serve warm or cold spread on the slices of crusty bread and sprinkled with freshly chopped parsley.

★ **Variation**

You can replace the calf's liver with lamb's or pig's liver in equal measure.

TOMATO & CHEESE TART

Serves: 8–10

Prep: 30–35 mins, plus chilling

Cook: 4 mins

Ingredients

125 g/4½ oz strong white flour

125 g/4½ oz self-raising flour

½ tps salt

125 g/4½oz chilled butter

1 egg yolk

4 tbsp cold water

oil, for greasing

rocket salad, to serve

Filling

8–9 tomatoes, peeled, deseeded and cut into eighths

150 g/5½ oz coarsely grated Emmenthal cheese

4 eggs

100 ml/3½ fl oz double cream

2 tbsp chopped fresh oregano or marjoram

1 tbsp chopped fresh chives

salt and pepper

Method

1 Sift the flours and salt into a bowl, then sift again to mix thoroughly. Dice the butter and work it into the flours, rubbing between your fingertips and thumbs until the mixture resembles dry sand. Beat together the egg yolk and water, and stir into the flour mixture with a fork. Once the dough starts to clump, knead very lightly to form a compact ball. Wrap in clingfilm and chill in the refrigerator for at least 30 minutes.

2 Preheat the oven to 160°C/325°F/Gas Mark 3. Lightly grease a 28-cm/11-inch loose-based tart tin. Roll out the pastry very thinly and use to line the tin. Pass a rolling pin over the top of the tin to trim off surplus dough. Using the side of your forefinger, press the dough into the corner of the tin to raise it slightly above the rim. Line the pastry base with greaseproof paper and weigh down with dried beans, making sure they go all the way to the edge. Bake blind for 15 minutes.

3 Arrange the tomato segments in the pastry case in concentric circles. Sprinkle the grated cheese evenly over the top. Beat the eggs lightly, then stir in the cream, oregano, chives and salt and pepper. Mix well, then pour into the pastry case. Return to the oven and bake for 20–25 minutes, until puffy and golden. Serve hot or warm with a rocket salad.

TOMATO TOASTS WITH THREE TOPPINGS

Serves: 4–6   **Prep: 25–30 mins**   **Cook: 5 mins**

Ingredients

12 thick slices
country bread

12 tomatoes, peeled,
deseeded and diced

8 garlic cloves,
finely chopped

about 350 ml/12 fl oz
olive oil

salt and pepper

Ham & caper topping

2 slices ham,
cut into thin strips

8 capers, drained
and rinsed

Chorizo & cheese topping

8 slices ready-to-eat chorizo

55 g/2 oz Manchego or
Cheddar cheese, sliced

2 pimiento-stuffed
olives, halved

Anchovy & olive topping

12 canned anchovy fillets in
oil, drained

4 anchovy-stuffed
green olives

Method

1 Toast the bread on both sides. Meanwhile, place the tomatoes in a bowl and break up with a fork, then mix in the garlic. Spread the tomato mixture evenly over the toast, season to taste with salt and pepper and drizzle with the olive oil.

2 For the ham and caper topping, arrange the strips of ham in an 'S' shape across 4 of the toasts and place a caper in each curve of the letter 'S'.

3 For the chorizo and cheese topping, place 2 slices of chorizo on each of 4 of the remaining toasts and top with the cheese. Garnish with an olive half.

4 For the anchovy and olive topping, curl 3 anchovy fillets into circles, place on the remaining 4 toasts and put an olive in the centre of each.

★ Variation

Experiment by leaving out and substituting various toppings. Anchovies and chorizo aren't to everyone's taste so could be replaced with more subtle ingredients.

INDEX

INDEX

256

This edition published by Parragon Books Ltd in 2015
LOVE FOOD is an imprint of Parragon Books Ltd

Parragon Books Ltd
Chartist House
15–17 Trim Street
Bath BA1 1HA, UK
www.parragon.com/lovefood

ISBN 978-1-4723-6463-0

Printed in China

Cover photography by Ian Garlick
Introduction by Anne Sheasby

Notes for the Reader
This book uses both metric and imperial measurements. Follow the
same units of measurement throughout; do not mix metric and imperial.
All spoon measurements are level: teaspoons are assumed to be 5 ml,
and tablespoons are assumed to be 15 ml. Unless otherwise stated, milk
is assumed to be full fat, eggs and individual vegetables are medium,
and pepper is freshly ground black pepper. Unless otherwise stated, all
root vegetables should be peeled prior to using.

Garnishes, decorations and serving suggestions are all optional and not
necessarily included in the recipe ingredients or method. Any optional
ingredients and seasoning to taste are not included in the nutritional
analysis. The times given are an approximate guide only. Preparation
times differ according to the techniques used by different people
and the cooking times may also vary from those given. Optional
ingredients, variations or serving suggestions have not been included
in the time calculations.

Vegetarians should be aware that some of the ready-made ingredients
used in the recipes in this book may contain animal products. Always
check the packaging before use.